Praśna Upaniṣad

Rediscovering Indian Literary Classics
(ISSN - 0972-0111)

1. Taittirīya Upaniṣad: With the Original Text in Sanskrit and Roman Transliteration; by Muni Narayana Prasad. (ISBN 978-81-246-0014-6)

2,4-5. Bṛhadāraṇyaka Upaniṣad: With Original Text in Roman Transliteration. English Translation and Appendices; by Nitya Chaitanya Yati; Vol. 1: Madhu Kāṇḍa; Vol. 2: Muni Kāṇḍa; Vol. 3: Khila Kāṇḍa. (ISBN 978-81-246-0008-5)

3. Kena Upaniṣad: With the Original Text in Sanskrit and Roman Transliteration; by Muni Narayana Prasad. (ISBN 978-81-246-0034-4)

6. Muṇḍaka Upaniṣad: With the Original Text in Sanskrit and Roman Transliteration; by Muni Narayana Prasad. (ISBN 978-81-246-0105-1)

7. Kaṭha Upaniṣad: With the Original Text in Sanskrit and Roman transliteration; by Muni Narayana Prasad. (ISBN 978-81-246-0110-5)

8. Praśna Upaniṣad: With the Original Text in Sanskrit and Roman transliteration; by Muni Narayana Prasad. (ISBN 978-81-246-0129-7)

9. Aitareya Upaniṣad: With the Original Text in Sanskrit and Roman transliteration; by Muni Narayana Prasad. (ISBN 978-81-246-0142-6)

10. Śrī Dakṣiṇāmūrti Stotram of Śrī Śaṅkarācārya; with the commentary Tattva Prakāśikā; by Swami Tattvavidananda Saraswati; Edited by Puppala B. (ISBN 978-81-246-0210-2)

11. Āditya Hṛdayam: With the Commentary Tattvaprakāśikā; by Swami Tattvavidananda Saraswati (ISBN 978-81-246-0231-7)

12. Vāstuśāstra: Ancient Indian Architecture and Civil Engineering — Retrospects and Prospects; by Rahul Kumar Altekar (ISBN 978-81-246-0246-1)

13. Gaṇapati Upaniṣad: With the Commentary Tattvaprakāśikā; by Swami Tattvavidananda Saraswati (ISBN 978-81-246-0265-2)

14. Life's Pilgrimage Through the Gītā; by Swami Muni Narayana Prasad (ISBN 978-81-246-0310-9)

15. Chāndogya Upaniṣad: With the Original Text in Sanskrit and Roman transliteration; by Swami Muni Narayana Prasad (ISBN 978-81-246-0374-1)

16. Īśāvāsya and Māṇḍūkya Upaniṣads: Translation and Commentary by Swami Muni Narayana Prasad (ISBN: 978-81-246-0492-2)

Rediscovering Indian Literary Classics, no. 8

Praśna Upaniṣad

with the original text in Sanskrit and Roman transliteration

Translation with
an Extensive Commentary
by
Swami Muni Narayana Prasad

PRINTWORLD
Publishers of Indian Traditions

Cataloging in Publication Data — DK
[Courtesy: D.K. Agencies (P) Ltd. <docinfo@dkagencies.com>]

Narayana Prasad, ***Muni*****,** 1938-
Praśna Upaniṣad.
(Rediscovering Indian literary classics; no. 8)
Includes bibliographical references (p.)
ISBN 13: 9788124601297

1. Upanishads. Praśnopaniṣad — Commentaries.
2. Hinduism — Sacred books. I. Upanishads.
Praśnopaniṣad. English & Sanskrit. Selections. II. Title.
III. Series: Rediscovering Indian literary classics; no. 8.

ISBN 13: 978-81-246-0129-7 **ISBN 10: 81-246-0129-1**
First published in India in 1999
Second impression in 2012

Published and printed by:
D.K. Printworld (P) Ltd.
Regd. office : *'Vedaśrī'*, F-395, Sudarshan Park
(Metro Station: Ramesh Nagar)
New Delhi - 110 015
Phones : (011) 2545-3975; 2546-6019; *Fax* : (011) 2546-5926
E-mail: indology@dkprintworld.com
Web: www.dkprintworld.com

Preface

All Upaniṣads teach the one and only secret wisdom, the very meaning of the word *upaniṣad* being 'secret wisdom'. Through words the Upaniṣads try to impart knowledge of that which is beyond words. Known as *Bhrahma-vidyā* (wisdom of the Absolute) and *Ātma-vidyā* (wisdom of the Self), Upaniṣadic teaching leads to one becoming fully aware of one's own self-content, which is none other than that of the world, and thus, it leads to seeing oneself identified with everything. Experincing oneself in everything, and everything in oneself, marks the attainment of this wisdom, its ultimate benefit being the sense of absolute Freedom.

The Western mind may consider Upaniṣadic teaching as being flawed by one major inadequacy — that it nowhere enjoins one to love others. While in one sense this appears to be a valid charge, we must keep in mind the fact that the Upaniṣads are part of a culture of seeing everything as part of one's self. Even the daily routines of life are to be based on this awareness, so that one would not even think of eating without sharing one's food, as the saying, *atithi devo bhava* (the guest varily is god) indicates.

There are certain scriptures called *Dharma-Śāstras* that give special emphasis not only to loving others, but lay down detailed moral instructions as well. But they are relegated to a secondary position, as living a morally sound life guided by wisdom, without imposed moral codes, is considered higher than a life lived following formally structured moral codes.

Different Upaniṣads attempt to shed light on the one wisdom, answering different questions, some concisely (e.g., *Māṇḍūkya*, *Īśa*, *Kena*) and some elaborately (e.g., *Bṛhadāraṇyaka*, *Chāndogya*,

Kaṭha, Praśna, Muṇḍaka). The words of the Upaniṣads are to be seen as wrappings; what is contained in them wrapped is the true wisdom. To open the wrapping and see for oneself what is in is the task of a keen student, an earnest seeker, to be done on his own.

It is possible that readers should wonder, as a Western friend did, why I should write a new commentary when there already exist numerous commentaries, beginning with Śaṅkara's. My only answer is that I have been inspired to try a hand at applying the master-key provided by my teacher, Nataraja Guru (chief disciple and successor of Sri Narayana Guru), in unlocking the word-packages of this Upaniṣad to allow me as well as others to glimpse the mysterious secret hidden within. The methodological devise that has been made use of in this commentary, as in my other commentaries, is that of dialectics, which the *Bhagavad Gītā* calls *Yogabuddhi*.

The *Prasna Upaniṣad*, in solving the problem of origin of beings, presents the philosophy of *Brahma-vidyā*, as answers to the six questions asked to Pippalāda by six seekers. Each leads to the other, and so on till the last one which reaches back to the first one, thus completing a full circle. These questions and answers deal with such topics as the actualities of begetting children on the one hand, and the sublimity of the non-dual Reality, the *param puruṣa* (Supreme Person) of sixteen *kalā*s, on the other. The first question is centred on the procreation of beings through mating, the second on the pre-eminence of *prāṇa* in living beings, the third on the Self as the source of *prāṇa*, the fourth on the functional states of the Self, the fifth on meditating *AUṀ*, the sixth on the Supreme *puruṣa* from whom arise all things.

Attempt has been made in this commentary to unravel the riddle-like statements and contexts of the Upaniṣad in the light of the meta-logic of *yoga-buddhi*. This work is the result of the joint effort of a group of research scholars and inmate students of Narayana Gurukula. Each stanza has been privately pondered on by each of them followed by a group discussion. The ideas thus clarified were systematised and then put in writing, first in the Malayalam Language, my mother tongue, and then rendered into

English. Mrs. Kala Remesh Krishnan of Bangalore edited it simply out of her love for wisdom and the Narayana Gurukula Movement. All of us in this group are thankful to Messrs D.K. Printworld for their willingness to help these ideas reach the hands of those who are looking for new paths into the world of Upaniṣadic wisdom.

Jan. 31, 1999 **Swami Muni Narayana Prasad**

Contents

॥ ॐ ॥

Peace Invocation

शान्ति पाठः

ॐ भद्रं कर्णेभिः शृणुयाम देवाः भद्रं पश्येमाक्षभिर्यजत्राः।
स्थिरैरङ्गैस्तुष्टुवाꣳसस्तनूभिर् व्यशेम देवहितं यदायुः॥

स्वस्ति न इन्द्रो वृद्धश्रवाः स्वस्ति नः पूषा विश्ववेदाः।
स्वस्ति नस्ताक्ष्र्यो अरिष्टनेमिः स्वस्ति नो बृहस्पतिर् दधातु॥

ॐ शान्तिः। शान्तिः। शान्तिः॥

oṁ bhadraṁ karṇebhiḥ śṛṇuyāma devāḥ
bhadraṁ paśyemākṣabhir yajatrāḥ ।

sthirair aṅgais tuṣṭuvām̐ sas tanūbhir,
vyaśema devahitaṁ yadāyuḥ ॥

svasti na indro vṛddhaśravāḥ
svasti naḥ pūṣā viśvavedāḥ ।

svasti nas tārkṣyo ariṣṭa-nemiḥ
svasti no bṛhaspatir dadhātu ॥

oṁ śāntiḥ । *śāntiḥ* । *śāntiḥ* ॥

AUM May we, with our ears hear that which is auspicious, O Gods.
And may we, habitually offering oblations, see with our eyes that which is auspicious.
With strong bodies, singing your praises, may we live out our span of life destined to us by the gods.

May Indra of mature learning bestow well-being on us.
May Pūṣā (the sun), the knower of all, bestow well-being on us.
May Tārkṣya (Garuḍa), the annihilator of danger, bestow well-being on us.
May Bṛhaspati bestow well-being on us.

AUṀ Peace ! Peace ! Peace!

Guru: Let us begin our study of the *Praśna Upaniṣad* with the Peace Invocation.

Seeker: Why?

G: The Peace Invocation may be considered a prayer for an unhindered and successful completion of the study. It is customary in India to invoke God or one's Guru at the beginning of a serious work for its fruitful completion.

S: Why is the same Peace Invocation repeated at the close of the Upaniṣad? Is it necessary that a prayer should be made after the completion of the work?

G: The Peace Invocation at the end may be seen as an expression of thankfulness in having completed the work. It could also be gathered from the repitition of the same invocation at the beginning and end that the sense of fruitfulness attained is what was intended. Another deeper philosophical meaning also could be construed of it.

S: What?

G: An Upaniṣad reveals the ultimate meaning of life. A problem concerning ourselves and the world is here demanding resolution, and the search ends only after attaining a clarity of vision concerning life as a whole. It is not merely a difinitive answer that we finally get, but the question itself vanishes in the clarity of all inclusive vision. A discriminating student, on finishing the study of an Upaniṣad, discovers that the problem emerging at the beginning and its becoming irrelevant at the end, are two facets of the teaching, thus returning to where it began. This is implicit in repeating the Peace Invocation at the beginning and end of the Upaniṣad. The inclusion of Peace Invocations in Upaniṣad also has another reason.

S: What is it?

G: Don't you know that India in ancient times had the *gurukula* system of education?

S: Yes.

G: A *gurukula* is a school, often located in some forest where a teacher and a few students lived together. The students assembled in classrooms each morning after their daily ablutions. Minds, diverted to other matters till that moment, needed to return to the teachings. The Peace Invocation was a prayer made together in their effort to concentrate on what the *guru* was about to teach. The *guru* began after they had prepared themselves in this manner.

S: Why is the word *śāntiḥ* repeated thrice?

G: Peace is the one value that everyone aspires to. In life we encounter seemingly irresoluble problems that make life miserable. Such causes of suffering have been classified into three by our *ṛṣis*: self-created sufferings, those caused by other beings and those caused by fate, called *ādhyātmika duhkha, ādhibhautika duḥkha* and *ādhidaivika duḥkha*.

S: What is the nature of *ādhyātmika duḥkha*?

G: Many of our sufferings have their origin in ourselves. For example, a person, while alone, thinks of something desirable. Then an urge to possess it arises and they begin to strive to possess it. If something happens to obstruct it, the person begins to feel a deep hatred towards the obstruction. In the course of life this hatred leads to disasters. Such suffering is not caused by anything or anyone else. This self-caused suffering is known as *ādhyātmika duḥkha*, *ādhyātmika* meaning self-related and *duḥkha*, suffering.

S: What is *ādhibhautika duhkha*?

G: These are afflictions caused through no fault of one's own but of other beings.

S: And the last one, *ādhidaivika duḥkha*?

G: Suffering caused neither by oneself nor by others, which happens as if willed by God, is known as *ādhidaivika duḥkha*. Natural calamities, famine due to drought or flood, and the like come under this category.

We long for relief from all three kinds of suffering and so it is *śāntiḥ* repeated thrice in all Peace Invocations.

S: Going through the text of the Upaniṣads I noticed that they do not all begin with the same Peace Invocation.

G: You are right. Different Peace Invocations go with different Upaniṣads. The Upaniṣads under the same Veda generally have the same Peace Invocation, but there are cases of exception.

S: Basically what is the difference between various Peace Invocations?

G: Some of them belong purely to the Vedic background of rituals and worship of gods, the present one being perhaps the best example. Certain others are overwhelmingly charged with mystical, philosophical insight. For instance, the Peace Invocation of the *Īśa Upaniṣad* and the *Bṛhadāraṇyaka Upaniṣad*:

> That is plenum; this is plenum.
> From Plenum, plenum emerges
> Plenum from plenum subtracting
> Plenum alone remains!

S: How is its Sanskrit original?

G: *auṁ pūrṇam adaḥ pūrṇam idam*
pūrṇāt pūrṇam udacyate
pūrṇasya pūrṇam ādāya
pūrṇam evāvaśiṣyate,
auṁ śāntiḥ śāntiḥ śāntiḥ

Let us now study the details of the present Peace Invocation.

S: Which Veda is this Upanisad appended to?

G: *Atharvaveda*. This Peace Invocation has a peculiarity of its own.

S: What is it?

G: It consists of two prayers adopted from the *Ṛgveda*.

S: The Vedas, as I understand, give primacy to rituals and the Upaniṣads to pure wisdom. How can, then, Vedic prayers be adopted as part of an Upaniṣad?

G: The *śānti pāṭha* is not actually meant to teach any philosophical principle as in the Upaniṣad proper. Derived from the Vedic culture, the Upaniṣads cannot entirely forgo their Vedic origin. Instead, these magnificent superstructures of wisdom are erected on the strong foundation of Vedic culture. These Vedic stanzas adopted as Peace Invocation of the present Upaniṣad, are not only philosophically meaningful but also adds to its poetic beauty.

S: The Upaniṣads, as I know, are in the form of dialogues. Are they imaginary, or have they actually taken place?

G: It could be either way. What is more important for us is that the philosophical vision revealed in the dialogues should become ours.

In fact, all the Upaniṣads are not in the form of dialogues. A number of these dialogues are rather dramatic, while in some others, characters do not come on the scene at all. Only questions and answers are presented. In some cases only the answer is given and the question remains behind the scene. The *Praśna Upaniṣad* however is a dialogue.

S: Why should this Upaniṣad, appended to the *Atharvaveda*, adopt Ṛgvedic verses as its Peace Invocation?

G: A little bit of history is needed here. Orthodox Vedism, does not recognise the *Atharva* as a Veda, and refers to the Vedas as *trayī*, meaning an aggregate of three, and those who follow this tradition call themselves *trivedī*s. Those who accept the *Atharvaveda* as the fourth are known as *caturvedī*s; *catur* means four.

Vedic culture is thought to have been brought to India by the Āryans from Central Asia. The first three Vedas belong to the fold of Āryan culture, while the *Atharvaveda*, though of a later date, derives from the pre-Āryan culture of India, and is therefore unacceptable to Orthodox Vedism.

In general these Vedas are predominantly comprised of rituals, whereas the most important and succinct of the Upaniṣads are those appended to the *Atharvaveda*. For example, *AUṀ*, the one sound that represents the essence of Indian Spirituality, is elucidated in the

Māṇḍūkya Upaniṣad.

S: Does it mean that the *Atharvaveda* stands for a different culture and way of thinking?

G: Though such an assessment is not out of place, the general character of the *Atharvaveda* is similar to that of the other three. It originated from the people of a pre-Āryan culture, at a later date. The *Atharvaveda* and the literature appended to it, doubtless has a substantial role in the cultural history of India.

S: What was that role?

G: The other three Vedas had, scattered through its vast body, indications of a clear vision of the fundamental Reality of life. Such precious teachings were rediscovered, collated and presented later in a revised form in the *Atharvaveda* and the literature appended to it, the *Praśna Upaniṣad* one of them. The one underlying Reality taught here could also be called God.

S: Why is it that, instead of being a prayer to that one God, the present Peace Invocation is addressed to various gods? It doesn't seem to agree with the Upaniṣadic line of thought either.

G: Have we entered the Upaniṣad proper?

S: Not yet, *guru*.

G: Upaniṣad is also known as Vedānta, the end of Veda. Veda means knowledge, Vedānta its end. From where should we enter the end of knowledge?

S: From its beginning.

G: What is the origin of Vedānta?

S: The Vedas.

G: The gods adored here are of the same Vedic culture from where we are yet to enter the Vedānta concept of one God or Reality. It is therefore quite befitting that the Peace Invocation at the beginning of an Upaniṣad is addressed to the Vedic gods.

S: Does that mean that such Vedic concepts are admitted by the

Upaniṣads?

G: The great masters of the past had never resorted to the method of denying any of the prevailing ideas. Instead, they revised and restated them, giving them a broader dimension, in the brighter light of which the former sense became irrelevant. This method known as dialectical revaluation in the history of thought, has been prevailing since ancient times.

S: The first prayer in this Invocation is for hearing that which is auspicious. How is this to be understood in the light of what you said just now?

G: Is there anyone who prays to God for something inauspicious?

S: No.

G: Do you think, our efforts alone will ensure auspiciousness in life?

S: I don't think so. Even the best of our efforts do not necessarily result in what we hope for.

G: Events in life, it is evident, do not occur according to our plans and wishes. Then, who is it that controls them?

S: I don't know. Yet I know that in spite of all its changes and transformations, the world continues to exist as a well ordered system. It is to be presumed therefore that some knowingness controls everything.

G: Phenomena, countless in number and nature, are mostly inexplicable. The ancient *r̥ṣis* of India conceived of one Absolute Being that underlies and controls all through, functioning in different ways in each. The specific way in which Reality functions in a particular phenomenon was considered its presiding deity (*devatā*), each called a *deva* (god), literally that which in essence is brightness, for knowledge we know is an experience of brightness and not of darkness. The poetically minded *r̥ṣi* invokes such gods for that which is auspicious.

S: Is it enough that we relegate to gods the responsibility of bringing about auspiciousness?

G: No, we should prepare ourselves also for receiving such favours.

S: How should we prepare ourselves?

G: By having the ability to discriminate between good and bad, the will to stand by the good, and the self-restraint not to be allured by the inauspicious.

S: Do you mean, only those who have this will-power and self-restraint will be eligible for favours from the gods?

G: Yes, they alone are eligible; and they alone will have the mind to make such a prayer. The Peace Invocation could therefore be considered a prayer and an oath. Besides, this prayer is made not by an ordinary person, but by one who longs for that wisdom which alone is the ultimate and the most auspicious goal. The present prayer has implicit in it a clear notion of the goal of life, the determination to be firm and the self-restraint essential for its attainment.

S: The prayer here is evidently made by seekers of wisdom, but they have qualified themselves as those habitually offering oblations, which is an aspect of ritual and not of wisdom teaching. How is this apparent inconsistency to be understood?

G: The supplicants qualify themselves as *yajatras* (those who are of the habit of performing *yajñas* or offering oblations). The word *yajña*, has different connotations in the context of Vedic ritualism and of Vedāntic widsom. In the former context it means performing fire sacrifices for the blessings of the gods, but in the present Upaniṣad as well as in the *Bhagavad Gītā* the concept gains a new dimension of meaning.

S: How?

G: Are we not living here as part of total nature?

S: Certainly.

G: Can we separate ourselves from nature and have an independent existence?

S: Never.

G: Nature itself is in a constant state of change. Isn't it so?

S: Yes.

G: Is it not as part of the mutability of nature that we also constantly undergo changes?

S: Yes, of course.

G: Every change involves an event or a chain of events, and certain actions take place at every event: fire burns, water flows, wind blows, trees grow, and so on. Don't you think all our activities also form part of nature's actions?

S: I think, it must be so.

G: Who is then the real doer of our actions, we or nature?

S: Nature alone, it seems, is the doer of actions; our actions are merely part of nature's actions, which are without beginning or end. Yet don't we have the freedom to decide what to do and what not to do?

G: Yes, we do, but what functions in our using of the freedom we have is nature itself, we being part of total nature.

S: Do you mean that we do not perform any *karma* or action at all?

G: Properly understood, we do not have any *karma* of our own.

S: Then what about the idea of our *karma*s and their fruits to be enjoyed or suffered?

G: I should say it is the greatest of our misconceptions born of ignorance. All actions take place in nature; the doer, if any, must be nature itself. Our ignorance of this simple truth makes us think we are the doers of actions, and bearing their burden renders our life miserable. Can you tell me a way out of this human predicament?

S: I think I can. Just give back to nature what was wrongly taken as ours.

G: This giving back to nature what belongs really to nature, and not to us, is the *yajña* or scarifice acceptable in the wisdom context. It is this prayerful offering that was conceived by the ancient *ṛṣi*s as *yajña*. It became a central concept of the Vedas, but was later altered into elaborate rituals by priests. Thus it is those who consider their own life and its activities as offerings who are *yajatra*s of the wisdom context.

S: I had never thought of the word *yajña* to have such a profoundly philosophical implication. This prayer is addressed to *deva*s (gods). Does the concept of *deva* also have such a meaning?

G: Yes. *Devas* in the Vedic context are denizens of heaven, to be propitiated by humans through offerings of fire sacrifices. *Devas* in the philosophical sense, represent various functional aspects of the one consciousness that controls nature. The same functional aspects of consciousness in each of us are also sometimes called *devas* in the Upaniṣads.

S: Do you mean that our faculties of sight, touch, smell and so on could also be treated as *devas*?

G: Yes. The word *deva*, in the Upaniṣadic context, stands for the various functional modes of consciousness, individual as well as cosmic.

S: Who is it that is addressed, when praying to be able to hear 'that which is auspicious' and so on?

G: This, as we have seen, is both prayer and oath. As a prayer it is addressed to the unknown Reality that creates from itself the experience of hearing, seeing and so on; as a solemn oath it is a value-based direction given to one's own senses of hearing, seeing and so on.

S: But the senses merely engage their objects with no value orientation.

G: You are right. It is not the senses but the possessor of senses, the 'I'-sense, that is endowed with value notions. When value notions conducive to the realisation of the ultimate meaning of life guide our senses, it philosophically becomes equivalent to the attainment of god's blessings.

S: Are the sense-organs to be restrained from their natural functions?

G: No. The senses and the mind are to be allowed their natural functions. No spiritual goal is attained by restraining them by force. When a sense functions in its natural way, very often mind, getting overshadowed by the particular sense contact, intensely identifies with the concerned object and it clouds self-awareness. This should not happen. Instead, the attitude of being a dispassionate witness to the function of the senses has to be cultivated. We will then be able to maintain a balanced state of mind even when senses are engaged with objects; spirituality also gains a stable ground therein. In themselves, the functions of the sense are never a cause of suffering; it is the mind that matters. An equable mind clears the path to the ultimate goal of spirituality, and may therefore be considered a blessing or auspiciousness bestowed on us by gods or senses.

S: What is really meant by *bhadram* (auspiciousness)?

G: It literally means that which makes us happy, a sense fully in line with Vedism, along with its implied meaning, goodness. The Vedic hymns and rituals are aimed at happiness here and in the hereafter. But this happiness, dependent as they are on rituals, is a relative auspiciousness. There is another happiness, another auspiciousness, well-being and stability,which is dependent on nothing, experienced on realising the ultimate Reality in oneself, experienced both by the *guru* and the seeker.

S: Pleasures and pains, good and evil, are normal in life. Do you mean that those who have attained wisdom will have only good and pleasurable experiences?

G: No. They will, with a sense of detachment and equanimity, be capable of regarding pleasure and pain, good and evil, as unavoidable; neither overcome with pleasure nor overwhelmed by pain, they are able to remain in constant peacefulness — the absolute auspiciousness that is the aim of wisdom.

S: Why is it that ears and eyes alone are mentioned though the sense organs are five in number?

G: Man's principal contact with the world is through seeing and hearing. The two are considered, therefore, to represent all the five senses. But related to Upaniṣadic wisdom, it has a deeper implication.

S: What is it?

G: The attainment of wisdom culminates in the transformation of that which is *heard* into that which is *seen*.

S: Please explain.

G: How does a disciple attain wisdom?

S: By hearing the words of instruction of a *guru*.

G: Such hearing of instruction is known as *śravaṇa* is Sanskrit, simply meaning hearing. Do you think the seeker will remain satisfied with the hearing of those words?

S: No. He should ponder on them, and make clear to himself what was intended to be conveyed by the *guru*.

G: This pondering on what is heard, is known as *manana* which leads through meditation to the inner vision or *darśana*, (this last stage is known as *nididhyāsana*). *Darśana* is the Indian word for philosophy, meaning thereby that all philosophical enquiry reaches its finality in a clear vision of Reality. Vision is a function of eyes; what is visualised here is the inner content of what was heard from the *guru*. A philosophical certitude is thus the transformation of heard wisdom into a vision of Ultimate Reality — the most auspicious sight any eye can ever see.

S: The next part of prayer is for living out the assigned life-span, strong in body. I don't think the necessity of a healthy body needs any explanation.

G: I don't think so either, but the necessity of a healthy mind should not be overlooked. An unhealthy mind in an unhealthy body makes a miserable life.

S: Does that have any implicit meaning in the wisdom context?

G: The meaning there also is explicit. A person weak in mind and body will not find himself capable of philosophical speculations. Of course people have overcome physical disabilities with a sharp and willful mind. Some of the Upaniṣads, for this reason, emphasise the need for a healthy body and all essential material comforts as a basic value in human life. The *Taittirīya Upaniṣad*, for example, says,

> Let there be a youth, a good youth,
> Well read, full of aspirations, steady
> in mind and strong in body. Let this whole
> earth, full of wealth, be his.
> That is one human happiness. — (II.8)

S: Is this human happiness related in any way to the Supreme Happiness?

G: It may seem unrelated. But the above *Taittirīya* passage concludes with the portrayal of Supreme Happiness (*brahmānanda*) as this human happiness multiplied many times.

S: How can worldly happiness multiplied many hundred times be equal to *brahmānanda*?

G: Now it is difficult to go into its details. You could refer to the commentary on that Upaniṣad.*

S: Our life is impermanent, and it is not difficult to understand why one prays for the ability to spend one's assigned lifetime in seeing and hearing that which is auspicious and in praising God. Is there any other meaning?

G: The most auspicious thing one can aspire to in life is realising what is ultimately Real. One who has attained this goal sees himself as immortal, not different from the one birthless and deathless Reality. This is a goal attained only by a very few, as though by the grace of God. The present prayer therefore is also an invocation for the dawning of wisdom and for living in the light of it.

S: What is prayed for in the second part of this Peace Invocation is *svasti*. What does it mean?

G: It is a word of benediction usually uttered by *gurus* in blessing their disciples or when the elders of a family bless the younger members. Literally, it means 'a good or praiseworthy state of existence', *su*, meaning good or praiseworthy and *asti*, existence or state of being.

S: Who is Indra apart from being the chief of the gods?

G: Derived from the root *ind*, meaning 'to have supreme prosperity and controlling power', Indra means, the one possessing these (*indati iti indraḥ*). According to another derivation — *im drāti iti indraḥ* — from the root *im*, Indra means that reality because of which everything here is in a state of eternal flux. In both senses what is referred to is Absolute Reality, realising which brings about one's oneness with Indra. Indra in this context may be understood both as the man of wisdom (*jñānin*) and also as Absolute Reality, and *svasti* as the benediction of well-being conferred by wisdom.

S: How is Indra a *vṛddha-śravāḥ*?

---

* See our commentary of the *Taittirīya Upaniṣad*. A D.K. Printworld Publication.

G: *Vṛddha* means 'of matured growth', and *śravāḥ*, hearing or learning. Hearing the words of instruction from a *guru*, is called *śravaṇa*. Learning in general, even self-learning, especially of the scriptures, is also considered *śravaṇa*. One who had attained maturity in such a learning is called *vṛddha-śravāḥ* (one of mature learning).

S: Who is the *pūṣā* prayed to here?

G: *Pūṣā* is another name for the sun. Literally the word means nourisher (*puṣṇāti iti pūṣā*), who is also a wise one or *jñānin* and none other than Absolute Reality.

S: How is that so?

G: Wisdom enriches human life, it enriches the world. The epithet *viśva vedas* is also sometimes given to *pūṣā* in this sense.

S: What does that word means?

G: *Viśva* means the cosmos, the total. The one who sheds light in the entire cosmos, the sun is known as *viśva vedas*, the one who knows or sees all. In the context of the humans, whosoever knows the total Reality is a *viśva vedas*, '*vedas*' meaning the knower.

S: Tārkṣya or Garuḍa, next invoked for well-being , is the bird-vehicle of Viṣṇu, the god who sustains. That the vehicle of a god is invoked, not god himself, for *svasti* sounds strange.

G: More than as the vehicle of Viṣṇu, Tārkṣya here is a symbol of resoluteness and prowess, two qualities without which it would be impossible to reach higher wisdom.

S: Why is he qualified as *ariṣṭanemiḥ*?

G: The word means one who is capable of keeping all obstructions outside the periphery of normal activities (*ariṣṭa*, obstructions; *nemi*, the outer rim of a wheel).

S: Who is the Bṛhaspati, last prayed to?

G: He is the *guru* of the gods. The word means, the lord (*pati*), of the expansive (*bṛhat*), or the one Reality that transcends and controls everything expansive.

S: That Indra, Pūṣā, Tārkṣya, Bṛhaspati, all signify one Absolute Reality is clear now. May we understand other Vedic gods also in the same sense?

G: Yes, different gods signify the same Reality in different ways. We shall have to digress a lot, if we go into details. For the present, let us confine ourselves to the *Praśna Upaniṣad*. Before concluding the scrutiny of the *śānti pāṭha* we have to take note of a subtle aspect not explicit in the text. The two sections of the Invocation are mutually complementary and compensatory.

S: No such complementarity is evidently seen.

G: Well, in the initial section, what was first prayed for?

S: To hear only what is auspicious.

G: How was Indra qualified at the beginning of the second section?

S: As the one of matured learning or hearing.

G: Don't you know that only one who is matured in wisdom through 'hearing' will attain what is really auspicious? The first prayer made in the first section and the distinctive characteristic of Indra of the second section are thus mutually complementary.

S: Yes, it looks so.

G: In the same way, the second prayer, is for seeing auspicious sights. Clear and distinct seeing is made possible by the sun, invoked in the second half of the Invocation. So too the third prayer in the first half is for a physically strong body and Tārkṣya invoked in the second half is the embodiment of resoluteness and prowess. Finally, Bṛhaspati, the *guru* of the gods, the one who ensures that the gods function as they are meant to, is invoked for overall well-being.

In the first section of the Invocation, the stress is one of the firmness required of the supplicant, while in the second section the emphasis is on gods' grace, both of which are essential if prayers are to be effective. Wisdom or *jñāna* also attains perfection where the seekers' will and God's grace conjoin.

First Question

प्रथमः प्रश्नः

ॐ सुकेशा च भारद्वाजः, शैब्यश्च सत्यकामः, सौर्यायणी च गार्ग्यः, कौसल्यश्चाश्वलायनो, भार्गवो वैदर्भिः, कबन्धी कात्यायनस्ते हैते ब्रह्मपरा ब्रह्मनिष्ठाः परं ब्रह्मान्वेषमाणा, एष ह वै तत्सर्वं वक्ष्यतीति, ते ह समित्पाणयो भगवन्तं पिप्पलादमुपसन्नाः ।। १ ।।

oṁ sukeśā ca bhāradvājaḥ, śaibyaś ca satyakāmaḥ, sauryāyaṇī ca gārgyaḥ, kausalyaścāśvalāyano, bhārgavo vaidarbhiḥ, kabandhī kātyāyanas te haite brahmaparāḥ brahma-niṣṭhāḥ paraṁ brahma-anveṣamāṇā, eṣa ha vai tat sarvaṁ vakṣyatīti, te ha samit-pāṇayo bhagavantaṁ pippalādam upasannāḥ ।। 1 ।।

Sukeśa son of Bharadvāja, Satyakāma son of Śibi, Gārgya grandson of Sūrya, Kausalya son of Aśvala, Bhārgava of the Vidarbha country, Kabandhi son of Kātya, all considering *Brahman* as the supreme goal, firmly intent on *Brahman*, seeking the highest *Brahman*, sacrificial fuel in hand, approached the revered Pippalāda, thinking, "He verily will teach us all".

Seeker: What is the relevance of the ancestry of the seekers in wisdom teaching?

Guru: To indicate that their ancestors were also seekers like them.

S: Why is that necessary?

G: Personal characteristics and natural dispositions, to a certain extent, are hereditary, a fact brought to light by modern genetics. These six seekers whose ancestors were also like them, may have a stronger inclination towards wisdom seeking.

S: Why are the seekers qualified as *brahma-paras*?

G: One who considers *Brahman* the highest value in life is a *brahma-para*. Whatever the vagaries of day-to-day life, for the *brahma-para*, the master interest is knowing the real in himself, and leading a befitting life. This is not an interest developed in all. To be satisfied with worldly pleasures and comforts is the course of human nature. We are often caught up creating an impression of being happy rather than in really being happy. If asked, "Are you happy?" then the person may unwrap a bundle of unending complaints, stories of difficulties and problems, trials and tribulations. The reason for this is that the person's life is not guided by the question, "What is the meaning of life?"

S: What does make one think of the meaning of life?

G: For some it is a natural thing. For others disasters, bringing abrupt and total change in the way of life, prompt them to ask this question.

S: May be the reference to the lineage of the seekers indicates their belonging to the former type.

G: Yes, such a nature is evident in their willingness to stay with Pippalāda for another year, and also in the questions they ask.

S: Why did they then need the help of a *guru*?

G: This was necessary because, though they knew that the ultimate meaning of life was *Brahman*, they did not know what that *Brahman* was and therefore, were in search of it (*brahma-paras*).

S: There are people who know that life has a meaning and that it has to be realised, yet do not find time to spend on it, sometimes cursing themselves for it. Are they to be treated also as *brahma-paras*?

G: No. They do know what they really need, yet lack in the resoluteness to pursue it. Why are they in such a predicament?

S: Worldly interests draw them away from what they are really in search of. They are not mentally strong enough to put a check on themselves.

G: An ability to think properly and to have proper value notions are thus not enough; a firmness on the part of the seeker to adhere to these values at all costs is also essential. The *Bhagavad Gītā* calls this firmness *dhṛti*[1] classified as *sāttvika* (pure clear), *rājasa* (affective-passionate) and *tāmasa* (dark inert). To have such a firmness, sometimes requiring a sort of drastic and uncompromising attitude towards oneself, is a rare gift in life. That the present seekers have that firmness is suggested by the word *brahma-niṣṭhāḥ* (firmly intent on *Brahman*). A clear notion of the ultimate goal of life and the firmness to keep to it are mutually supportive.

S: All the six seekers are in search of the knowledge of *Brahman*, but none of them does ask Pippalāda the *guru* to teach them *brahma-vidyā*. Why is it so?

G: It is the answers rather than the questions of this upaniṣad that make it clear what the seekers were after — *Brahman*. Whom should one approach when such burning problems terment them?

S: A person who knows Reality and has no more any such problems in life.

G: Not easily available, such a master has to be sought out, as these six did, indicated by the compound word *param brahmānveṣamānāh* (seeking the supreme *Brahman*. Finally they did find a *guru* in Pippalāda. Wisdom blossoms where seeker and knower conjoin, each Upaniṣad an instance of it.

S: The seekers are seeing Pippalāda for the first time, but expect him to teach them everything. How can they have such an expectation of a stranger?

G: A real seeker or disciple cannot and will not see a stranger in a real *guru*.

S: Why not?

---

1. *Bhāgavad Gītā*, XVIII. 33-5.

G: The seeker, burning with the desire for wisdom, will go only to the person who, he is sure, knows what he is in search of. The *guru*, real man of wisdom, will also be awaiting with similar desire, for a competent disciple, so as to impart to him what he knows. This inner urge in the *guru* meets with the wisdom-desire in the seeker and the intimacy between the two attains maturity and perfection. The seeker immediately feels he will get from this *guru* what he was in search of.

S: Why are they with sacrificial fuel in hand?

G: Disciples in India customarily, when they first approach their *guru*, keep a small bundle of firewood in hand (*samit-pāṇi*, *samit* meaning firewood and *pāṇi* meaning hand). *Samit*, which means any firewood, here stands for the particular kind of firewood called *camatā* used for fire sacrifices. *Guru*s usually live in hermitages (*āśrama*s) where fire-sacrifice is part of daily routine; student-inmates of an *āśrama* in principle consider even their life an offering to *Brahman*. A newcomer with firewood in hand, indicates his willingness to treat his own life as fuel to be burnt in the wisdom sacrifice. The willingness to live in the hermitage with humility and participate in all the routine activities with full dedication, is also implied in this gesture.

Wisdom is often compared to fire. The nature of any fire flame depends on the fuel burnt. When it is one's self that becomes fuel, the fire of wisdom, will blaze with the radiance of the Self.

Above all, on seeing a young man approaching an *āśrama*, firewood in hand, no one has to ask him what the purpose of his visit is, the firewood signifies that he is a wisdom seeker. Here also, Pippalāda, on seeing the six seekers, did not ask them the purpose of their visit. He, without making any enquiry, asked them to live with him for an year with full dedication, as we will see in the next stanza.

S: Who was Pippalāda?

G: According to one tradition, he was a direct disciple of Vyāsa, the collator of the four Vedas. Vyāsa, it is held, selected four out of his chief disciples and entrusted each with the responsibility of propagating one of the Vedas; the *Ṛgveda* for Sumanta, the *Yajurveda* for Vaiśampāyana, the *Sāmaveda* for Jaimini, and the *Atharvaveda* for Pippalāda. This tradition of course does not fully agree with the historical view.

S: *Pippala* as I know is a kind of berry, and *ad* means to eat. Could we then take Pippalāda as an eater of berries?

G: Yes. *Pippala* is a delicious berry and Pippalāda thus become a poetic name for pleasure seekers, but the present Pippalāda eats the berry of wisdom, the six seekers here wanting to partake of it.

The seekers will ask six questions, one answered in each chapter. At first, these questions may appear random, but a closer look will reveal their structural coherance and perfection bringing to full relief the wisdom of the Absolute (*brahma-vidyā*). The six seekers thus represent six stages in a methodic unveiling of *brahma-vidyā*.

तान् ह स ऋषिरुवाच — भूय एव तपसा ब्रह्मचर्येण श्रद्धया संवत्सरं संवत्स्यथ, यथाकामं प्रश्नान् पृच्छत, यदि विज्ञास्यामः सर्वं ह वो वक्ष्याम इति ॥ २ ॥

tān ha sa ṛṣir uvāca — bhūya eva tapasā brahma-caryeṇa śraddhayā saṁvatsaraṁ saṁvatsyatha, yathā-kāmaṁ praśnān pṛcchata, yadi vijñāsyāmaḥ sarvaṁ ha vo vakṣyāma iti ॥ 2 ॥

To them that seer said: Live with me another year with austerity, *brahmacarya* and faith. Then ask what questions you will. If we know we shall indeed tell you all.

Seeker: Firewood in hand, the seekers' intention was evident to Pippalāda, but he does not make any other enquiry; instead straight-away asks them to live with him another year; a strange behaviour!

Guru: Pippalāda might have made such primary enquiries but these are irrelevant to the wisdom context.

S: Why were they asked to spend one more year with him?

G: They were asked not simply to live with him, but to live with *tapas*, *brahmacarya* and *śraddhā*. A master may at firt glance make out the intention of the newcomer, but still not be sure of his worthiness. Wisdom imparted to an unfit seeker will not be fruitful and may prove even harmful.

S: What is *tapas*? Stories have been heard of *ṛṣis* going in seclusion to perform *tapas*, but here the seekers are asked to live with *tapas* in the presence of the *guru*.

G: Literally, the word means 'heating up'. The austere practice of *tapas* we usually hear of is also a sort of self-heating process, to make one pure enough to know oneself.

S: What is the necessity of it in self-enquiry?

G: Another *tapas*, undergone by *brahman* or *ātman*, resulting in the creation of the world, of living things, and of the seeker himself, has also to be kept in mind. *Brahman*, according to some of the major Upaniṣads, had the primordial desire to become many. It underwent *tapas* with this desire, resulting in the emergence of the world, as if through the hatching of an egg. This is described in detail, for example, in the *Aitareya Upaniṣad*. The seeker, who is the tail end of this creative unfolding, has in him the creative urge to retrace his own origin, which is *Brahman*, the Reality, and this needs a *tapas* on his part, the very *tapas* undergone by *Brahman* for his creation. One *tapas* is meaningless without the other.

S: *Tapas* as a spiritual discipline is thus one's intense effort to find one's own source in oneself?

G: Yes, and for that reason *brahmacarya* is also appended to *tapas*.

S: What is *brahmacarya*?

G: Usually understood as observing celibacy, it really means walking on the path of *Brahman*; *carya* means walking on a prescribed path. For those who know that *Brahman* is the underlying Reality in every-thing, knowing It is the highest value in life. Whatever the vagaries of day-to-day life, they will find a way to make all things conducive to this ultimate goal. Such a *carya* or way of life is truly *brahmacarya*, and one who is on that path, not necessarily celibate, is called a *brahmacārin*. As for celibacy, it is not clear at least from this Upaniṣad, whether the seekers, or even Pippalāda himself, were celibates. The possibility of his having a family cannot be ruled out. The very life process of the seekers, in search of wisdom ever willing to dedicate themselves to this one goal, attains in principle the status of *brahmacarya*. In asking them to undergo one more year of disciplined life, the *ṛṣi* was testing the intensity of their quest for wisdom.

S: How is *brahmacarya* related to *śraddhā*, which I know as the keen attention we pay to anything, for example, to this lesson?

G: *Śraddhā* is more than keen attention, as of students, to a lesson taught. It is the full faith a seeker has in the words of wisdom of his own *guru* as well as in the recorded words of the *guru*s of the past. This is one of the essential prerequisites for a disciple to achieve fruition of wisdom.

S: Does it mean that he has to blindly believe in what the *guru* says?

G: Attaining wisdom is the goal of the seeker in approaching a *guru* who, he believes, knows what he is in search of. That the present seekers had this belief was evident from the very first stanza.

A *guru* imparts his wisdom through words, which may not be transparent to the seeker as soon as heard. The latter has to ponder on it, perhaps for a long time with full faith in its truthfulness. After a long period of cogitation and meditation on those words, everything may become transparent to him like a revelation. Without that faith, he would have been unable to ponder on those words and to reach that final transparency, which alone makes him realise how his initial faith was essential. *Śraddhā* is therefore considered one of the most important prerequisites in the search for truth and is not mere dogmatic belief of any religious significance.

Hinduism, if a religion at all, is not based on dogma, neither does it demand of its followers belief in dogmas. If at all it demands anything, that is *śraddhā*. *Śraddhā* thus serves only as the spring board for a methodic self-enquiry.

S: The importance of *śraddhā* is clear to me now. Is the one year that the six seekers are asked to be with Pippalāda, enough for any seeker?

G: No set rule exists on this matter. What the seekers are asked even here is to live 'another' year, not 'one' year, implying thereby their having led a similar life before. What will be taught by the *guru* after this one year would constitute merely the *śravana* part of their enquiry, to be followed by *manana* and *nididhyāsana*, needing perhaps a further extension of the same kind of life. Attaining finally, the final transparency of Reality, one does not feel like giving up that disciplined life, finding it the applied aspect of the transparent wisdom. Not meant for practising for a fixed duration, this way of life has thus to be pursued initially and will become spontaneous eventually.

S: Why were they then asked to live with him one more year only?

G: A *guru*, seeing a newly arrived disciple, his appearance, his demeanor, his mode of behaviour, can approximately guess how long he will take to receive the wisdom teaching. Pippalāda, in the present case, estimated that they would need to be with him for a year. There are cases of *gurus* asking their disciples to live with them for twelve years or even a lifetime.

S: Finding them intent on *Brahman*, why were they not taught straightaway?

G: Nothing is wrong in doing so, but allowing some time to pass, puts the questions and the questioners in perspective. The questions they ask a year later may not be the ones they would ask straightaway. Living with the *guru* a year may clarify many subtle factors hitherto unknown, sometimes changing altogether the nature of their doubts. The original doubts may perhaps vanish and new ones, deeper in significance, arise, or doubts may even vanish altogether, leaving no more questions.

The *guru*, moreover, is yet to become familiar with the personal characteristics of the seekers, an inevitable prerequisite for effective and fruitful teaching, each person having to be taught as his personality requires. Getting that familiarlity takes some time.

There are people who go to masters and ask questions, expecting an immediate answer. They want to go home by the return bus or train. Wisdom is not to be taught in such a hurry, its secrets get revealed only to those who are willing to wait patiently, even for years. A *guru* will, before teaching, verify the seeker's patience and dedication. A dedicated seeker will be willing to spend even a whole lifetime. Such disciples are traditionally known as *antevāsins*, literally, those who dwell along with, doing personal services for the *guru* a natural part of such a life.

S: Why are the seekers allowed to ask questions 'as they will'?

G: A year's staying with the *guru* would make them capable of more mature thinking and questioning. The freedom given them in the choice of questions will induce them to refrain from asking trivial or irrelevant questions.

S: Why does Pippalāda say, he will answer them 'if he knows'?

G: No *jñānin* claims to be one. Wisdom makes one humble. True wisdom is a secret unknown to those who claim to know it, but known to those who know they do not know it. This mystical state is described in the *Kena Upaniṣad* (II.3); a touch of it is seen in these words of Pippalāda too.

True wisdom is an inner awakening and its meaning cannot be contained by any word. This wisdom reveals what is ultimately Real, which emanates as everything including words. Words, emanated as they are from the Real, can never make the Real its own meaning. So its finality is not taught through words but through silence. Whether a disciple is to be taught through words or silence is decided by the *guru* on the merit of each case, on the maturity of the disciple. All these are implicit in Pippalāda's words that he would teach 'if he knows'.

S: Pippalāda's words 'if I know' and 'shall tell you all' seem to contradict each other.

G: This too shows the peculiarity of true wisdom. 'If I know' does not really mean that he does not know. He is simply reserving the right to decide whether to teach them or not, and the method of teaching — through words or silence.

The six lived with Pippalāda and they still had questions after a year.

अथ कबन्धी कात्यायन उपेत्य पप्रच्छ, भगवन् कुतो ह वा इमाः प्रजाः प्रजायन्त इति ।। ३ ।।

atha kabandhī kātyāyana upetya papraccha, bhagavan, kuto ha vā imāḥ prajāḥ prajāyanta iti ।। ३ ।।

Then Kabandhi son of Kātya, approaching him asked: "Venerable Sir, whence verily are all these creatures born?

Seeker: Kabandhi, the last one mentioned in the first verse, comes up with his question first. Why is it so?

Guru: Sukeśa's name was mentioned first, but he will ask the final question. This reversal of order is meaningful. With the final question and its answer, the teaching of the Upaniṣad reaches its finality; so the last question is the most important one and should be asked by the most learned of the seekers. Their names were given in the order of their grade of learning. The least learned asks the most primary of questions, and so his question comes first and the same order is followed throughout.

S: Were all the six present when Kabandhi asked his question and Pippalāda answered?

G: It is to be presumed so, though not mentioned specifically. The hermitage of a *guru* is a public place; he never teaches privately. The answer to questions, though asked by individuals, is meant for all. In the present case, you will notice, each new question arises from the answer given to the previous one, which is an indication of the presence of all the six.

How does a person, not well matured in thinking, consider the world?

S: He takes everything he sees as real.

G: If he has an alert mind, what kind of doubts arise in it?

S: As to how all these came into being, from where, and so on.

G: That is Kabandhi's question. The Upaniṣad thus begins from inquistiveness arising out of ordinary experience, each new question leading to a new realm of higher thinking, till the final question, at the zenith of the teaching, provides an integral vision of the Real.

S: According to the little understanding I have of philosophy, it tries to answer two basic questions, 'Who am I'? and 'Whence this world'? Kabandhi asks only one of them.

G: Don't you live as an integral part of the world?

S: Yes.

G: If so, your knowledge of the reality underlying the world, your knowledge of the origin of the world, is also your knowledge of yourself. Conversely, your knowledge of yourself is also your knowledge of the reality of the world. Enquiry about one leads to knowledge of both. For this reason in the Upaniṣadic contexts, the two questions are not asked together.

S: How do the two methods — asking the two questions together and asking one of the two — differ?

G: To attempt to answer set questions is merely an exercise meant to satisfy one's intellectual curiosity, whereas the visualisation of Reality portrayed in the Upaniṣads is of a different order. We live, and the reality underlying us is also a living one, not merely a fixed idea or theory. Life being a progression, the experience of Reality has in turn to be an experience of progression. No progression can be from everywhere to everywhre. It has to be from somewhere to somewhere. All of Reality is to be directly experienced in and through this progression, and that is how a living experience of Reality is the goal of all Upaniṣads. It is the full satisfaction of living fully aware of the meaning of life.

The enquiry here, though apparently concerning the origin of beings in the world, also concerns ourselves, we and the world being not two.

S: What is meant by *prajā*?

G: Literally it means that which is born. Everything that has come into being is a *prajā*.

S: The Upaniṣads, as I know, teach the birthless and deathless Reality, but the question asked here presupposes birth and death. Why this inconsistency?

M: The present chapter, as I already told you, looks at the basic problem from the common man's point of view, where birth and death are taken for granted. The answer will lead the seeker to higher realms of Reality.

S: We know all beings are born of mating of males and females. I don't see anything philosophical in it.

M: Besides recognising the birth of beings by that biological process, this chapter directs us to the Supreme Principle that has set everything in this world for the perpetuation of life in such a way. Pippalāda begins his answer in the next stanza with a direct reference to this principle, called Prajāpati in Upaniṣadic terminology.

तस्मै स होवाच — प्रजाकामो वै प्रजापतिः, स तपोऽतप्यत, स तपस्तप्त्वा, स मिथुनमुत्पादयते रयिञ्च प्राणञ्चेति, एतौ मे बहुधा प्रजाः करिष्यत इति ॥ ४ ॥

tasmai sa hovāca — prajā-kāmo vai prajāpatiḥ, sa tapo 'tapyata, sa tapas taptvā sa mithunam utpādayate rayiñ ca prāṇañ ceti, etau me bahudhā prajāḥ kariṣyata iti ॥ 4 ॥

He (Pippalāda) said to him: Prajāpati, verily, was desirous of offspring. He underwent *tapas*. Having undergone *tapas*, he produced the couple *rayi* and *prāṇa*, expecting them to produce offspring of various kinds for him.

Seeker: Who is Prajāpati?

Guru: *Prajā* means created beings and *pati* lord; thus *prajāpati* (another name of Brahmā the Creator) is the lord of created beings.

A volition works behind all acts of creation and is figuratively called the Lord of Creation. *Viśva-vīrya* (cosmic urge) is the word preferred by Narayana Guru. *Brahman*, the primeval Reality, conceived as throbbing with this inner urge for the creation of the world, is named Prajāpati.

S: Is Prajāpati's desire for offspring similar to our desires in day-to-day life?

G: Yes, in one sense. All our desires are for specific ends; Prajāpati's desire, nature's urge for new beings to emerge, is simply an innate urge for self-expression, thus more fundamental.

S: Please explain.

G: One Reality, Pure Consciouness in essence, underlies all this world. Our direct experience of that Reality is in the form of I-consciousness, the consciousness that is conscious of itself. The Real is called *sat* and consciousness *cit*; thus *sat* is *cit* in essence.

Consciousness does not remain inert, it is always in some functional state, wanting to see for itself what potentials are hidden within itself. This urge incessantly transforms itself as everything, as all the world, actualising the contentment of self-expression (*ānanda*). This is comparable to the satisfaction felt by children in their play of creating and destroying many things for the sheer joy of it. Prajāpati's desire for offspring is nothing but this inner urge.

S: Is the *tapas* undergone by Prajāpati with the desire for offspring, similar to the *tapas* of the seekers?

G: Yes, the seekers undertook *tapas* in order to *realise* the all-potent Reality within; the *tapas* of Prajāpati was for *actualising* inner potential. Some extent of heating or utilisation of energy is unavoidable in creation or manufacture. In the worldly sense, the heated and the applier of heat are different, whereas in Prajāpati's *tapas* the two are the same. Hence, it is called the *abhinna-nimittopādāna-kāraṇa* (the undifferentiated material and incidental causes) of the world.

S: Why did Prajāpati, instead of creating the world right away, produce the couple *rayi* and *prāṇa*?

G: All living beings originate, from the mating of males and females. Pippalāda's answer as this chapter ends, leads us to the very same point, in the context of an over-all scheme for the world. This macro-scheme also has inherent in it a basic couple principle in perpetual embrace. The coming stanzas will refer to many such couples, beginning here with *rayi-prāṇa*. *Rayi* and *prāṇa*, thus stand for the cosmic aspect of the couplehood that ensures a ceaseless progression of life.

S: What are *rayi* and *prāṇa*?

G: *Rayi*, mostly used in Vedic literature to denote material wealth, is used in this Vedāntic context in a more abstract and general sense, to mean the material aspect of life. *Prāṇa* stands for the vital principle of life, abstract and general.

S: Prajāpati, the Lord of Creation, should be capable of creating directly. Why did he choose the indirect way of creating through *rayi* and *prāṇa*?

G:Unconsciously we mistake Prajāpati for a personal God, and the present doubt is a result of it. *Brahman,* the one Absolute Reality, charged with the inner urge for creation, is Prajāpati. Any event that happens in nature is thus an act of Prajāpati. That Prajāpati creates everything and that everything happens in the natural course of events, mean the same. The couple-principle inherent in all events, more poetically and dramatically is conceived of as emerging from Prajāpati who expects the two to produce offspring of various kinds. Even the innate urge in males and females to mate and procreate, is a part of Prajāpati's desire. *Prāṇa* and *rayi* are merely two mutually reacting functional modes of nature. In short, Prajāpati creating the world and couples producing offspring are not two successive stages of creation. They are the same, the former more religiously conceived and the latter more scientifically.

आदित्यो ह वै प्राणो, रयिरेव चन्द्रमा, रयिर्वा एतत् सर्वं यन्मूर्तं चामूर्तं च, तस्मान्मूर्तिरेव रयिः ॥ ५ ॥

āditiyo ha vai prāṇo, rayir eva candramā, rayir vā etat sarvaṁ yan mūrtaṁ cāmūrtaṁ ca, tasmān mūrtir eva rayiḥ ॥ 5 ॥

Prāṇa is the sun indeed, and *rayi* the moon. All that is materialised and non-materialised is *rayi* indeed. Whatever is concrete is therefore *rayi*.

Seeker: Equating *prāṇa* and *rayi* with the sun and the moon, instead of clarifying, makes things even more vague. As a couple, the two are to be suggestive of male and female, a relationship not at all relevant between sun and moon.

Guru: *Rayi* and *prāṇa*, we have noticed, have a very broad significance. The Sāṁkhyan concept of *prakṛti* (nature) and *puruṣa* (person), and the *yin* and *yang* of Taoism are somewhat similar to these; they also resemble the modern concepts of matter and energy. At the most earthly level, they are male and female. The following stanzas will outline various levels at which the duality of *prāṇa* and *rayi* are to be understood, the sun and the moon simply first among them.

S: A prior knowledge of these levels of duality, I feel, will help us appraise the coming stanzas.

G: The sun and the moon are the dual aspects that emerge from Prajāpati first. The year is then seen as Prajāpati, here the darker and brighter halves of the year are the dual aspects. The two paths supposedly taken by departing souls, are also conceived as pertaining to this context. Next the month is conceived as Prajāpati, the brighter and darker fortnights forming the couple. Then the solar day is visualised as Prajāpati, where day and night are the couple. Coming closer to the topic of procreation, it says, by mating during the day one loses one's *prāṇa*; mating at night is equivalent to *brahmacarya*. Food is finally visualised as Prajāpati and sperm and ovum as the *prāṇa-rayi* couple emanating from him. The cyclic progression of life is such that brighter and darker aspects alternate which is true even of our mental state. *Prāṇa* and *rayi* thus stand for this twin aspect of life, and Prajāpati for the overall creative progression.

S: How do the sun and the moon come on the scene?

G: As celestial bodies shining at day time and night, the sun and the moon are poetic representations of the brighter and darker aspects of life.

S: *Prāṇa*, in the usual sense, is the vital function in each of us. How can it be symbolised by the sun?

G: The two are not symbol and symbolised, but rather, both are symbols. Though we are aware of our vital organic functions, vaguely called *prāṇa*, no one has any clear idea of it, no one knows how it reaches nourishment and vitality to each of our body cells, how the sensory system functions, or how the different systems together make a living entity—all of which we assume to be the functions of *prāṇa*. To say that all this is the work of *prāṇa*, does not mean that we know of a *prāṇa* apart from these functions. *Prāṇa* is really nothing more than a name symbolising all the vital functions together.

So too with the sun. This celestial body, emanates all the energy we need for our sustenance and growth, yet we are in the dark as to how it works. The process of the sun's constant emitting of energy and our constant absorption of it is a great mystery. In relation to each individual being, this process is *prāṇa*, and related to the cosmic system, it is symbolised by the sun. Both *prāṇa* and the sun are thus symbols.

S: Of the *prāṇa* and *rayi*, I think the former is non-material and the latter material. How can both materialised and non-materialised be *rayi*? Then it says, "Whatever is concrete therefore is *rayi*". I think this needs clarification.

G: The original words for 'materialised' and 'non-materialised' are *mūrta* and *amūrta*. *Mūrta* means any material entity with a specific tangible form. No tangible form remains constant; everything changes, and new forms emerge. The material that undergoes all these changes has no distinct and tangible form of its own and thus is *amūrta*, the opposite of *mūrta*. *Mūrta* and *amūrta* are thus two aspects of material existence, the realm where any concretisation is possible in the worldly sense, and in that sense it is said, "Whatever is concrete (*mūrta*) is therefore *rayi*."

The next stanza shows how the sun energises the total system of life.

अथादित्य उदयन् यत् प्राचीं दिशं प्रविशति तेन प्राच्यान् प्राणान् रश्मिषु सन्निधत्ते। यद्दक्षिणां यत्प्रतीचीं यदुदीचीं यदधो यदूर्ध्वं यदन्तरा दिशो यत्सर्वं प्रकाशयति तेन सर्वान् प्राणान् रश्मिषु सन्निधत्ते ॥ ६ ॥

athāditya udayan yat prācīṁ diśaṁ praviśati, tena prācyān prāṇān raśmiṣu sannidhatte । *yad dakṣiṇāṁ yat pratīcīṁ yad udīcīṁ yad adho yad ūrdhvaṁ yad antarā diśo yat sarvaṁ prakāśayati, tena sarvān prāṇān raśmiṣu sannidhatte* ॥ 6 ॥

Now then, the sun on rising, enters the eastern horizon, thus bathing all life in the east with his rays. So too, on his illumining the directions of the south, the west, the north, below, above, in between, he bathes all living beings with his rays.

Seeker: Apart from what we know of the role of the sun in our life, I don't make out anything exceptional in this stanza.

Guru: It appears so unless read along with the next two stanzas. How *prāṇa* and *rayi* had their origin in Prajāpati, we have seen, as also how *prāṇa* could be equated to the sun. The present stanza shows in what sense *prāṇa* and the sun are equal.

S: Is it not enough that we understand the next stanzas as a continuation of the present one?

G: No. To understand a stanza keeping in mind what follows in the next stanzas is something different. Comprehending any sequence in these stanzas needs such a study.

S: O.K. Yet I don't understand how the sun can rise in all directions and illumine all directions.

G: The text does not say the sun rises in all the directions, it rises in the east, but illumines all directions. Still, it is figuratively not wrong to conceive of a sun that rises in all directions. The sun that rises in the east leads us gradually to the conceptual sun that energises all life everywhere, like *prāṇa* everywhere in the body, rising everywhere. The sun, we know, is the symbol of cosmic *prāṇa*, the dynamism by which the cosmic system lives, symbolised by the sun's rays bathing all living things in its rays.

S: Normally we think of directions as four in number. Here in the Upaniṣad we see a different system of counting directions.

G: Besides the four horizontal ones, Indians count above and below also as two directions, thinking of the material world three-dimensionally. Sometimes the north-east, the south-east, the south-west and the north-west are also counted, making the number of directions ten.

स एष वैश्वानरो विश्वरूपः प्राणोऽग्निरुदयते। तदेतदृचाभ्युक्तम् ।। ७ ।।

विश्वरूपं हरिणं जातवेदसं परायणं ज्योतिरेकं तपन्तम्।
सहस्ररश्मिः शतधा वर्तमानः प्राणः प्रजानामुदयत्येष सूर्यः।। ८ ।।

sa eṣa vaiśvānaro viśva-rūpaḥ prāno'gnir udayate ।
tad etad ṛcābhyuktam ।। 7 ।।

viśva-rūpaṁ hariṇam jāta-vedasaṁ
parāyaṇaṁ jyotir ekaṁ tapantaṁ ।
sahasra-raśmiḥ śatadhā varta-mānaḥ

prāṇaḥ prajānām udayaty eṣa sūryaḥ ॥ ८ ॥

This sun, the Vaiśvānara assuming every form, life and fire, rises (everyday). This very truth has been declared in the *Ṛgveda* thus:

This Sun, who has everything for its form, constituted of rays, the all knowing, the goal (of all), the sole effulgence, the giver of heat, the possessor of thousands of rays, existing in hundreds of ways, the life of all creation, rises.

Seeker: Who is the Vaiśvānara mentioned here? Another Vaiśvānara, the name of our consciousness in its functional state of wakefulness, is known to me, as described in the *Māṇḍūkya Upaniṣad*.

Guru: The Vaiśvānaras of these two Upaniṣads belong to different contexts and have different connotations.

S: How do they differ?

G: The *Māṇḍūkya Upaniṣad* deals with the Self as Consciousness in its four alternating states of waking (*jāgrat*), dreaming (*svapna*), deep-sleep (*suṣupti*) and the fourth (*turīya*); Vaiśvānara being the name given to the Self in its waking state. The creation of beings is the problem dealt with in the first chapter of the *Praśna Upaniṣad*. We know how *prāṇa* and *rayi* emerged from Prajāpati. After defining *rayi* in Stanza 5, *prāṇa* is described in Stanzas 6, 7, and 8 and as part of it comes Vaśvānara as an epithet of *prāṇa*. The usage of the word is clearly in two different contexts, in two different senses. Any serious study of a particular field of enquiry will have to clarify many points and problems within its frame of reference. Mixing up of such contexts (called *prakaraṇa*s), instead of clarifying things, will make things more ambiguous, a failing that had much endangered Vedāntic thought. We have to be very cautious of it in our enquiry.

S: Why is the sun of the last verse called Vaiśvānara here?

G: Used generally to mean that which is common with all human beings, the Supreme *Brahman*, and the sun, Vaiśvānara is a compound word formed of *viśva* and *nara*. *Viśva* means that which excludes nothing, and *nara*, one who can bring anything under his control. The word in the present context means, one who is in control of everything that is *rayi*, whether distinct or indistinct. It is nothing but the cosmic aspect of *prāṇa* equated to the sun in the last verse.

S: How does this vital power assume the form of the world (*viśva-rūpa*)?

G: Each epithet used here has a significance of its own. Calling it simply *prāṇa* would not reveal to us what was visualised by the *ṛṣi*. The *prāṇa* gained a cosmic dimension in the sun of the last stanza, and in the seventh stanza it gains a deeper metaphysical dimension as pervading and assuming every *rayi* form. Whatever be the form of the world, the *prāṇa* assumes that form by being the vitality pervading it.

This insight is not claimed by the *ṛṣi* as his own; he quotes a Ṛgvedic passage in support of what he visualises.

S: Do you mean that even minerals are pervaded by *prāṇa* and thus have life?

G: That the mineral kingdom does not have life is one of our presumptions. What the Upaniṣads teach is that everything, including the mineral world, is a manifestation of the primeval Substance, Pure Consciousness. Modern science also comes to a similar conclusion. Guy Murchie, in his book *The Seven Mysteries of Life* demonstrates how even a grain of sand is imbued with life.

S: *Prāṇa* also seems to be a keyword in this Upaniṣad. What does it actually mean?

G: It is a word derived from the root *an*, meaning, respiratory function, and the prefix *pra* means 'in the proper way'. In the Upaniṣad, the word is used with different connotations in different contexts. The wide range of its meaning, as far as this Upaniṣad is concerned, will become clear as we proceed.

S: Are *jīva* and *prāṇa* the same?

G: *Jīva*, equivalent to the English word soul, is not a word generally cherished by Upaniṣadic *ṛṣi*s. Literally it means the respiratory function of an organism (*jīva prāṇane*). It is not an invisible spirit that supposedly leaves the body at death, though such an idea has become fixed in the minds of people. Adding to this confusion, the word *ātmā* has also come to be treated as a synonym of *jīva*. All this was a result of the attempt of the scholars of Indian thought to systematise the transparent visions of seers into schools of philosophy. Disentangling them will be a hard task, but we shall try as best we can.

S: Is there any way out of this mess of ideas?

G: Yes there is. Delving deep into the mystical vision of the Upaniṣadic *ṛṣis*, without relying on secondary textbooks of Vedānta, might help. The *ṛṣis* do not see soul and body as two entities, one getting into or leaving the other, but as the subtlest and grossest facets of *ātmā* or I or Self-existence. *Ātmā*, translated as Self, thus is that reality which manifests itself both as soul and body. Even with respect to our body the idea we maintain is not fully correct.

S: How?

G: We think that the body has skin for its outer limit. But consider the air we breathe in: without it our body cannot exist even for a moment. Thus it forms part of our physical body, not only when it is within the body, but without too; with no air surrounding the body it would perish. The air around the body as part of the body, extends endlessly; our physical body also thus extends endlessly. This extensiveness is related with the element air. But body is constituted of other elements also — earth, water, fire, space. Our physical body then has to be thought of as being as extensive as the world itself. Thus, I, the Self, in each of us extends between soul, the subtlest aspect of existence, and the endless physical world. In other words, 'I', the Self, is the underlying reality that assumes the apparent forms ranging from soul to the endless cosmic system.

S: I never thought of my own existence as so extensive; I have to be very cautious to use the word 'I'. Why are all these equated to fire?

G: When *prāṇa*, one of the dual aspects born of Prajāpati, was equated to the sun, did you notice that, heat and light, the most apparent characteristics of the sun, were not taken into account?

S: No?

G: The sun was considered there as that which bathes all beings with its vitality, thus giving predominance to its all-pervading character. The same *prāṇa* was then considered as Vaiśvānara and Viśvarūpa, and finally as fire where heat and light alone are what matters.

Another functional difference between the sun and fire is also meaningful here. With the sun what was important was its bathing all beings with its rays, i.e., its all-pervading nature, whereas with fire its rising itself is the meaningful factor. The words *agnir udayate* of the original, mean, fire rises. Rising up is particularly meaningful in the context of the creation of the world — the problem we are dealing with in the present chapter. All the Upaniṣads consider the world as emanating or rising from one Reality as the expression of its own invincible creative urge. Each epithet thus has its own significance: *prāṇa* signifies inherent vitality in each being, the sun signifies all-pervasiveness, and fire, self-emanation. *Prāṇa*, the counterpart of *rayī* is thus the creative principle that inheres all these characteristic.

S: Do you think, fire being one of the five basic elements of nature is of any significance here?

G: Yes, it is. Each of the five elements has its own distinguishing quality: sound is the quality of space, touch of air, form of fire, taste of water, smell of earth; each element also possesses qualities of the elements previous to it; thus earth has all the five qualities. Of these, fire is distinguished by its quality of form. The all-pervasiveness of the sun and vitality of *prāṇa* have no form of their own. The fire principle is essential for the emergence of the world with form — Viśvarūpa. Giving shape to anything we know always requires some application of heat. So too, the sun and *prāṇa*, by themselves abstract, attain the form of the world because of the fire already inherent in them.

S: The bodies of living beings are generally warm; when dead, i.e., when *prāṇa* ceases to function, they become cold. Could this phenomenon be understood as related to the fire principle we are discussing?

G: Yes, it could be. The function of *prāṇa* is physically felt as the warmth of the body, only its degree varies in various beings.

S: The intention of the *ṛṣi* is almost clear, it seems. Is there anything more to be noticed in the Vedic verse quoted as Stanza 8?

G: The quoted verse is an elaborate version of the context of the previous verse. Though certain additional peculiarities are also notable.

S: Is the epithet *hariṇaṁ* of any special significance?

G: The word means that which is constituted of rays. We know how the sun and rays are related. *Prāṇa* too, more than mere respiratory function, as the knowledge that makes it work as it does, is of the essence of light. So the word *hariṇaṁ* fits in with both the sun and *prāṇa*.

S: What is *jātavedas*?

G: Another epithet of fire, though, it means one who knows everything born or the one who is born as a form of knowledge. Both this senses are significant here: as the witness of all that takes place in the form of birth and death in *rayī*, and as the one consciousness that assumes the form of all specific knowledge.

S: It is no wonder that such *prāṇa* is the final goal, the sole effulgence, the giver of heat.

G: The heat *prāṇa* possesses and gives and the heating undergone by Prajāpati resulting in the emanation of *prāṇa* and *rayī* are in essence not two; the heat of fire and the heat of the sun are also not to be excluded from *tapas*; all being merely various aspects of the same principle of *tapas*.

S: The rest of the epithets of *prāṇa* of Stanza 8, it seems, are quite understandable in the light of all these. I shall now try to summarise what I have understood so far:

Prajāpati, becoming desirous of offspring underwent *tapas*, resulting in the emergence of *prāṇa* and *rayī* — twin aspects analogous to the *puruṣa* and *prakṛti* of the Sāṁkhya system. *Rayī* is the realm of phenomenal becoming, of the appearances and disappearances of distinct forms. The pure vital principle, pervading all individual beings as well as the cosmic system, and witnessing all transformations, is the *prāṇa*, which flames like fire.

Are the upsurging function of *prāṇa* and the urge for higher knowledge in us related?

G: Of course. *Prāṇa*, you know, the sole effulgence and nothing but Pure

Consciousness, is not merely the respiratory function. Consciousness, in its function of knowing, always aims at higher levels of understanding. The phenomenal appearance of the world is one other outcome of the creative upsurging of Pure Consciousness. Yet another facet of the same creativity, closer to begetting offspring, is portrayed in the next stanza.

संवत्सरो वै प्रजापतिः, तस्यायने दक्षिणञ्चोत्तरं च। तद्ये ह वै तदिष्टापूर्ते कृतमित्युपासते, ते चान्द्रमसमेव लोकमभिजयन्ते, त एव पुनरावर्तन्ते। तस्मादेत ऋषयः प्रजाकामा दक्षिणं प्रतिपद्यन्ते। एष ह वै रयिर्यः पितृयाणः ॥ ९ ॥

अथोत्तरेण तपसा ब्रह्मचर्येण श्रद्धया विद्ययात्मानमन्विष्यादित्यमभिजयन्ते। एतद्वै प्राणानामायतनमेतदमृतमभयमेतत् परायणमेतस्मान्न पुनरावर्तन्त इत्येष निरोधः। तदेष श्लोकः॥ १० ॥

पञ्चपादं पितरं द्वादशाकृतिं दिव आहुः परे अर्धे पुरीषिणम्।
अथेमे अन्य उ परे विचक्षणं सप्तचक्रे षडर आहुरर्पितमिति ॥ ११ ॥

saṁvatsaro vai prajāpatiḥ, tasyāyane dakṣiṇañcottaraṁ ca । *tadye ha vai tad iṣṭā-pūrte kṛtam ity upāsate, te cāndramasam eva lokam abhijayante, ta eva punar āvartante* । *tasmād eta ṛṣayaḥ prajākāmā dakṣiṇaṁ pratipadyante* । *eṣa ha vai rayir yaḥ pitṛyāṇaḥ* ॥ 9 ॥

athottareṇa tapasā brahmacaryeṇa śraddhayā vidyayātmānam anviṣyādityam abhijayante । *etad vai prāṇānām āyatanam etad amṛtam abhayam etat parāyaṇam etasmān na punarāvartanta ity eṣa nirodhaḥ* । *tad eṣa ślokaḥ* ॥ 10 ॥

pañca-pādaṁ pitaraṁ dvādaśākṛtiṁ
diva āhuḥ pare ardhe purīṣiṇam ।
atheme anya u pare vicakṣaṇaṁ
sapta-cakre ṣaḍara āhur arpitam iti ॥ 11 ॥

The year verily is Prajāpati; emerging of him are two paths: the southern and the northern. Now, those who perform *iṣṭāpūrta* thinking of those rituals as of supreme value, they attain the world of the moon, certainly returning again. The sages desirous of offspring therefore take to the southern path. This, called the path of manes, is verily *rayī*.

But those who seek the Self by *tapas*, *brahmacarya*, faith and knowledge, they attain the world of the sun by the northern path. That verily is the abode of *prāṇa*s; that is the immortal; that is fearlessness; that is the final goal from where there is no return, for it is the termination. About that, there is this verse:

He is spoken of as the father having five feet and twelve forms, seated in the higher half of heaven full of water. Still others speak of him as an genius set on (a chariot) of seven wheels and six spokes.

Seeker: Why do we here take three stanzas together for our discussion?

Guru: In combination they present an overall picture of the cycle of life.

How beings are created is the question asked in this chapter; its answer is also on those lines, keeping to the general stance of Vedānta that creation is merely an illusory appearance. Creation admitted, it is one primeval reality, that has necessarily to be its cause. The couple *prāṇa* and *rayī* who emerged from Prajāpati, have to come down to the couplehood of man and woman to effect actual procreation, thus completing the picture. The present three verses together form the first step in this descending process.

S: Two paths, the southern and the northern, one leading to the world of the moon and the other to that of the sun, are mentioned here. How are these paths related to the sun and the moon, equated to *prāṇa* and *rayī*?

G: The couplehood of the sun and the moon was conceived at the beginning, foreseeing the couplehood of the two paths. As birth has been taken for granted here, death must also accompany it, leading thus to the problem of the hereafter. The *ṛṣi* was aware also of the ideas of after-life prevailing in the minds of common people who are unaware of the immortal Reality of life. The general belief was that those who performed rituals would, after death, travel on the path of manes (*pitṛ-yāna*) and reach the world of the moon, only to be reborn and return to this world. Those who considered wisdom as the highest value, were believed to pass along the path of the gods (*deva-yāna*) and reach the world of the sun and eventually the world of *Brahman*, never to return. The *ṛṣis* intention is not to give confirmation to such beliefs, but to correct them in the light of the absolutist vision of Reality of the Upaniṣad. This intention is implicit in conceiving of the sun and the moon, suggestive of the two paths, as forming a couple.

S: How is the year to be conceived as Prajāpati, the Lord of Creations?

G: We are now looking at creation, and, as a part of it, are bringing down to worldly level step by step the concept of couplehood. Every creation is an event. All events take place in time and space, with a cosmic as well as individual dimension. The cosmic couplehood of *prāṇa* and *rayī* gradually comes down temporally and spatially to the couplehood of the sperm and ovum of individual beings. Considering the temporal year as Prajāpati, is the beginning step of this process of descent. An year also has two halves, a brighter and a darker, in the place of *prāṇa* and *rayī*.

S: What is *iṣṭāpūrta*?

G: The ultimate goal of human life is to live liberated and fully aware of its meaning. Though all beings have an inner urge for liberation, not everybody can achieve it. The Vedic tradition holds that meritorious deeds will help to attain this goal. Such deeds called *karmas* are classified as *iṣṭa karma* and *pūrta karma*. Vedic rituals constitute *iṣṭa karmas* which include performing without fail all the fire sacrifices enjoined by the Vedas, to be austere, to be honest and honour brāhmaṇas. Doing such works beneficial to the public as digging public wells and tanks, planting shade trees, constructing places of worship, public feeding, etc., are called *pūrta karmas*.

S: Are such meritorious deeds done only during the darker half of the year?

G: Adherence to the darker path by those who are interested in rituals and pious deeds need not be understood to mean that they do such things only during the darker half of the year. Darkness signifies ignorance and the darker six months stand for the path of ignorance. Only the ignorant take to the path of rituals and pious deeds, and for that reason they are considered here as passing through the darker half of the year. Ignorant as they are, they believe they will reach the world of the moon after death and will return to this world again.

S: Should we then take the theory of rebirth as an accepted tenet of Vedānta?

G: Rebirth is meaningful only where birth and death are also meaningful. The method of approach adopted in this chapter admits birth as a fact and naturally rebirth also is discussed. It is not a basic tenet of Vedānta. That the real is birthless and deathless, is its basic teaching. There is no rebirth where there is no birth or death. The conclusive position of the teaching of the Upaniṣad can be seen when it is said,"Know him as the person to be known, so that death may not afflict you." This is the path of wisdom referred to in the 7th stanza as the northern path.

Whether birth, death and rebirth are real or unreal depends on how we understood ourselves. To be changeful is the nature of phenomenal becoming where appearance of new forms and disappearance of old forms is normal. What we call birth is the appearance of new forms of what is real, and death is the disappearance of old forms. A gold ornament can be melted and remoulded into any new form, still nothing happens to the gold, the reality in it. If the appearance of the form of the ornament is considered real then the disapperance of the form is its death, but if it is the gold-substance that is considered real, then nothing has happened to it whatever be the form it assumes.

In Vedānta, considering the apparent form as real, not knowing the indestructible reality in it, is called *avidyā* (ignorance). Knowing the indestructible substance as real, and the apparent changeful forms as unreal is called *vidyā* (knowledge). The substance was never born, will never die, is never reborn. Try to see yourself as of a gold-ornament. If you think of yourself as this visible, destructible form with various personal qualities as real, then death is inevitable. If, on the other hand, you think of yourself as the substance that has assumed the present form, then you were never born, you will never die. If you prefer to be ignorant, then birth is real, death is real, rebirth is real. If you prefer to be wise, then you were never born, you will never die, you are immortal. Now, which of the two do you prefer?

S: I prefer to be the ornament that knows 'I am gold'.

G: That is what Vedānta stands for. With this understanding, our day-to-day life gains a new stability despite its ups and downs.

S: Then what about reaching the world of the moon and returning?

G: It is simply an ignorant's concept of after-life. Some Upaniṣads do describe this process of leaving and returning in detail. The departed souls of the ignorant, they say, pass through the smoke of the pyre, through night, the darker fortnight, the darker half year, finally reach the world of the moon and then the world of manes (*pitṛloka*). They enjoy the fruits of their merits in that world for some-time, and as the merits run out fall back through rain to reach the earth. Cereals and vegetables assimilate this water and they in turn are consumed by men; the soul thus reaches semen which a man will deposit into the womb of his wife causing rebirth of the soul. This is the concept of the ignorant one who takes the unreal for the real. Such ideas in the Upaniṣads are not part of their teaching proper, but are meant only to show the delusion of the ignorant. The passage, "The sages desirous of offspring therefore take to the southern path" has to be pondered upon with all these in our mind.

S: A *ṛṣi* is a *jñānin*, a seer, a sage. How can he take to the darker path of becoming desirous of offspring?

G: Even Prajāpati became desirous of offspring; it does not reduce his greatness in any way. Here in this actual world we have *ṛṣis* in the place of Prajāpati; their desire for offspring in no way affects their eminence. *Ṛṣis* also live in this world of transience, in this world of *avidyā*. What differentiates them from the ignorant is that they are fully aware of the phenomenality of the world of *avidyā*. A real *jñānin* is an unattached witness to all happenings, knowing that nothing is constant in life. Oscillate as he does in between the worlds of *vidyā* and *avidyā* he will be fully aware of it, of what takes place in himself. A seer, transacting in the world of *avidyā*, also becomes desirous of offspring as part of the natural flow of life and he himself regards it as pertaining to the southern path.

S: How is *pitṛyāna* identified with *rayī*?

G: What *rayī* is we know — the inertial aspect of existence. Contrasting *pitṛyāna* and *devayāna* with *rayī* and *prāṇa*, the *ṛṣi* finds the former as inertial. All distinct entities are part of *rayī*. The *pitṛyāna* concept itself is equated to *rayī* here as though correcting indirectly the prevailing popular notion of rebirth. The idea of soul going to another world and then coming back itself is considered the inert or dark aspect of knowledge. It will become all the more clear on contrasting this path with the northern path (*uttarāyana*) in Stanza 10. The two paths are different in their goal. *Tapas*, *brahmacarya*, *śraddhā*, and *vidyā* are the means of attaining wisdom, the goal of the northern path. Vedic rituals and deeds of public benefit are the means in the case of the southern path. The two paths thus differ in their means also. There are more differences between the two paths.

S: What are they?

G: The prevalent belief related to the northern path is that the departed souls of *jñānins* rise up through the light of the pyre, passes through day, the brighter fortnight, the brighter six months, the world of the sun and finally reach the world of *Brahman* (*Brahmaloka*), to retaurn no more.

S: Yes. And those who take to the southern path are believed to return to the earth.

G: The concept of the soul's passage of no-return to *Brahmaloka* is also a construct of ignorance. *Jñānin* doesn't think of different worlds as real. The wise concept of no-return is of a different order. The gold-ornament analogy will help to clarify it:

"Like gold in an ornament, an immortal Substance underlies my being. My realising 'I am that Substance' makes me immortal here and now." This immortality is not something to be attained in another world after death; hence no more question of the here and the hereafter, going and coming. The present chapter conceives this experiential awareness of immortality as the world of the sun.

S: How does that experience become the experience of fearlessness?

G: Fear is an emotion common to all. But are you afraid of yourself?

S: No. My fear is always of something 'other' than myself.

G: When an ornament, realising 'I am gold', looks around at other ornaments, what does it see in all of them?

S: The same gold.

G: That means, it sees itself in them.

S: Yes.

G: Not afraid of myself, I will not fear 'others', once I am able to see myself in them.

S: That is true.

G: All fear ends when this distinction of 'I' and 'other' ends through attaining the wisdom of the Real. The *Bṛhadāraṇyaka Upaniṣad* even defines *Brahman* as 'fearlessness' — *abhayam vai brahma*.

S: What is the significance of the word *parāyaṇa*, translated as 'the final goal'?

G: The word means, that which can be depended on, relied on. To take the ornament-gold analogy, the substance an ornament has for its refuge is gold itself. Similarly, on finding the underlying Reality, the Self, as one's refuge, one experiences supreme happiness of eternal and unconditional secureness.

Parāyaṇa is also often used to signify final liberation (*mokṣa*) as the Supreme Goal. *Parā* means Supreme, and *ayaṇa* advancement; the word thus meaning, advancement towards the Supreme.

S: What is the termination mentioned here?

G: The original word *nirodham* means any lawful stop. When immortality and absolute fearlessness are attained, will there be anything more to aspire to in life?

S: No. One will then feel the contentment of having attained the final goal.

G: That means all enquiry terminates at that attainment.

S: Yes.

G: That is the termination mentioned here. It is a spontaneous ceasing of one's quest, not imposed by any one else. A quest makes one rely on some means; no means are needed when the final goal is attained. The termination thus is both of the quest for a goal and of the reliance on means. Relying on the northern path as means, and cessation of birth and death as ends are what we are concerned with presently; in both respects the attainment of immortality is a terminal point.

S: How is it that Prajāpati has five feet?

G: The year is the form of Prajāpati that we are concerned with at the moment. Indians divide an year into six seasons (*ṛtus*) just as four seasons are reckoned in the West. Of the six seasons, sometimes *śiśira* and *hemanta*, two stages of the cold season, are conjoined and treated as one, reducing the number of seasons to five, the five feet of the year-Prajāpati.

S: The twelve months should then be the twelve forms.

G: You are right.

S: How is Prajāpati seated in the upper half of heaven?

G: One Reality subsists all. It pervades the mythological realms of the three worlds: earth, heaven and hell, and the ever-expanding world of the modern scientific myth. This Reality, as the source of all creations, is the Prajāpati of this chapter.

The Vedas and mythology visualise Prajāpati seated in heaven, controlling all living beings. The Prajāpati of concern here is of a different order: of the wisdom contex of Vedānta. He is the Reality that transcends all the worlds. If there are three worlds, this Prajāpati is even above heaven, the topmost world. He is thus seated even above heaven; if within the three worlds, at the topmost region of heaven.

S: The *purīṣa* I know means dirt, but you translated it as 'full of water' Why this disparity in meaning?

G: It is true that *purīṣa* in ordinary usage means dirt, but in the Vedic context it stands for water, which is perhaps more true to its etymology. *Pṝ*, the root from which it is derived, means to reach and fill (*pṝ pūraṇe*), the basic quality of water. Reality or Prajāpati is poetically spoken of as full of water or as genius (*vicakṣaṇa*) seated on a chariot.

S: What does the genius riding a chariot with seven wheels and six spokes represent?

G: Poetical convention speaks of the year as being born of the sun.

S: It is not merely poetical imagery; it is a scientific fact as well.

G: It is an instance where scientific facts and poetical vision come together from two sides as it were, merging in the finality of wisdom.

The sun in his seven-wheeled chariot revolves round the world taking a year to complete the circle. The rolling on of the seven wheels makes seven parallel circles around the world, appearing like seven wheels which have the earth for their hub. *Cakra*, the original word for wheel, means that which reaches back where it began. Time sense thus is the result of the revolution of these cosmic wheels, one revolution making a year.

The six seasons are the spokes of the wheel. The Sanskrit word *ara* does not translate exactly as spoke, but means that part of the rim of the wheel where spoke is fixed. The number of spokes on the wheel of time depends on the unit of time you adopt, and need not always be six. You may imagine a slow moving giant wheel, like that of a bullock cart, to appreciate this poetic imagery fully. The wheel, say with six spokes, slowly roles on, each spoke hitting the ground at a time. Each spoke, no sooner it hits the ground than it goes behind giving way for the next one to come and hit the ground. With season as the unit of measurement, the revolution of the wheel of time looks very slow; but with moment as unit it appears very fast. It is the rolling on of the wheel of time with seasons or moments for its spokes, that makes the world move on, as the *r̥ṣi* Narayana Guru, who lived in the present century, conceived it.

S: I had not realised how great and sublime were the poetical imageries of our *r̥ṣi*s, where highly mystico-philosophical vision and precise scientific thinking merged and blended together.

The southern path described in Stanza 9 was equated to *rayī*, but the northern path detailed in the next stanza was not equated to *prāṇa* as one naturally expects. Why is it so?

G: The southern path, also called *pitr̥-yāna*, and *rayī*, go with ignorance. Only the ignorant consider birth and death as real. The passing of the departed souls through any path, southern or northern, is relevant only when death is considered real. Both paths are therefore ideas conceived by the ignorant. They think, after death, they will reach the *pitr̥-loka* through the southern path. A *jñānin*, according to them, after death, will reach the *Brahma-loka* through the northern path. A real *jñānin*, seeing no birth and death, thinks of no such paths. Nothing related to ignorance therefore goes with *jñānin*.

मासो वै प्रजापतिस्तस्य कृष्णपक्ष एव रयिः शुक्लः प्राणस्तस्मादेत ऋषयः शुक्ल इष्टं कुर्वन्तीतर इतरस्मिन् ।। १२ ।।

māso vai prajāpatis tasya kṛṣṇa-pakṣa eva rayiḥ śuklaḥ prāṇas tasmād eta ṛṣayaḥ śukla iṣṭaṁ kurvanti itara itarasmin ।। 1.2 ।।

Month verily is Prajāpati, emerging of it are the darker fortnight as *rayī* and the brighter fortnight as *prāṇa*. The *ṛṣis* therefore perform sacrifices in the brighter fortnight and others in the other fortnight.

Seeker: Prajāpati from being considered as the year is now being seen as the month. The absence of any detailed description of this month-Prajāpati may be to avoid repetition. Yet in one respect this Prajāpati differs from the Prajāpati as year.

Guru: How?

S: During the course of the year, *ṛṣis* desirous of offspring, performed their rituals and pious works in the darker half of the year. But the *ṛṣis* in this verse are seen to perform rituals in the brighter half of the month. How is this discrepancy to be explained?

G: *Iṣṭa karmas* (also called *iṣṭi*) in the Vedic context, are the rituals enjoined by the Vedas. Compared to the open and universal outlook of Vedānta, Vedic concepts and value notions are very narrow and limited. The Vedāntic way of wisdom has its own concept of *iṣṭa karmas*. The brighter fortnight represents wisdom; actions performed in its span are those befitting this wisdom. A man of wisdom views himself, as a transient manifest form that appears and disappears in the beginningless and endless creative self-unfoldment of the one eternal Reality. He sees himself filled with this Reality, even as a wave is filled with ocean. Whatever he happens to do as a part of this self-unfoldment of Reality, which we called nature, will be for the benefit both of himself as well as the total flow of life. Those *iṣṭa karma*s natural to the wisdom context, are a reflection of the brighter aspect of life.

अहोरात्रो वै प्रजापतिस्तस्याहरेव प्राणो रात्रिरेव रयिः। प्राणं वा एते प्रस्कन्दन्ति ये दिवा रत्या संयुज्यन्ते, ब्रह्मचर्यमेव तद्यद्रात्रौ रत्या संयुज्यन्ते ॥ १३ ॥

aho-rātro vai prajāpatis tasyāhar eva prāṇo rātrir eva rayiḥ। prāṇaṁ vā ete praskandanti ye divā ratyā saṁyujyante, brahmacaryam eva tad yad rātrau ratyā saṁyujyante ॥ 13 ॥

Day is verily Prajāpati, emerging of it, day time is indeed *prāṇa* and night indeed is *rayī*. Couple uniting in love by day time are dissipating their own *prāṇa*, couples uniting in love by night are practising *brahmacarya* indeed.

Seeker: I don't understand how the morality of mating during day time or at night fits in with the Prajāpati concept, now considered as the day.

Guru: We have been dwelling on the function of Prajāpati at different levels. His main function is creating beings, and couples are his tools. This universal principle of creation gets actualised in individual life through the process of sexual intercourse.

S: Why can't it be said simply that procreation occurs through the mating of male and female as willed by God?

G: That is the religious way, not of the way of an Upaniṣadic *ṛṣi* who is a philosopher and seer.

S: How do the two differ?

G: A religionist believes in an omniscient and omnipotent entity, often personified as God who wills and dictates everything in this world. He is the final judge of all human deeds. Whereas the philosopher-*ṛṣi* seeks to know the Reality underlying the world, which he finally realises as the Reality in himself . He thus realises his own non-difference from Reality.

S: How does the *ṛṣi* visualise the emergence of an individual being?

G: We have been learning of the principle of Prajāpati, from the primeval Prajāpati down to the day-Prajāpati. In the next verse *retas* (semen) is described as the common principle that links couples; *retas* here also represents the ovum. The principle of couplehood runs through the scheme of life embracing both its universal and individual aspects. Procreation through mating at night is thus visualised as an integral part of the total system of life.

S: The Prajāpati principle, running all through the present scheme, seems to represent non-dual Reality. If so, why adopt this round about way to come to it?

G: Since the frame of reference of this chapter takes creation for granted, it invariably has to be respected in the way thought is developed. The goal still remains arriving at an understanding of non-dual Reality. The idea of creation could as well be ignored; then the world and the beings in it are nothing but phenomenal appearances that constantly emerge in the one Reality as its own self-expression.

S: Why is having intercourse at day time considered self-destructive?

G: The general experience is that having sex at night is natural with human beings, causing no physical or mental tiredness. We don't know why it is so; just that the system works that way. Social life respects this as a moral code.

S: How is such a moral code related to the philosophical vision we are concerned with?

G: Any moral code is the applied aspect of some universal principle or natural phenomenon. Here also a universal principle is appraised first, then a universal code of conduct is stated. It could be argued that sex, natural to all living beings, can be had at any time, but that having sex at day time makes both the participants mentally and physically exhausted is an undeniable biological fact. The proper use of logical reasoning is not in denying actuality, but in understanding and making the best use of actuality. For the above reason, having sex at day time is condemned as equivalent to dissipating one's own *prāṇa*.

S: What *brahmacarya* is we know. How does having sex at night become equal to it?

G: Whatever is natural is part of the way *Brahman* functions. Whatever is done fully in line with such functions is *brahmacarya*. Couples, in having sex at night, are finding themselves in the creative urge of *Brahman*, an actual *brahmacarya*.

अन्नं वै प्रजापतिस्ततो ह वै तद्रेतस्तस्मादिमाः प्रजाः प्रजायन्त इति ।। १४ ।।

annaṁ vai prajāpatis tato ha vai tad retas tasmād imāḥ prajāḥ prajāyanta iti ॥ 14 ॥

Food indeed is Prajāpati, emerging of it is semen from which creatures here are born.

Seeker: Here we are finally at a fact known to everyone. Was all the story of Prajāpati, the year, the month, the day, all meant for teaching this?

Guru: Even the most common thing, we don't realise, is part of a vast, mysterious system. To have such an understanding about anything in this world means to make it part of *Brahmavidyā*, the knowledge of *Brahman*. The most common phenomenon of begetting children by mating is also seen here in the like manner. Though very common, no one thinks of the mystery behind this phenomenon.

S: What mystery is it?

G: There is nothing in it not mysterious. What get united in this process are sperm and ovum, two physical entities. The union of the male and female, also a physical event, has their free will behind it and they experience it not merely as a physical union but as an effulgence of great joy. The child born of this union has also his/her own physical existence, free will and potential to experience happiness. Do we know how all this happens? Is it explainable?

S: No, not at all.

G: Is this ignorance yours and mine, or is it an ignorance shared by all.

S: It is shared by everyone.

G: That it is unknowable is not the fault of those who try to think of it, but is part of the mystery of the world, and this is the new lesson taught here. The sexual union of the couple is thus a miniature version of the couple born of Prajāpati, even as any slight mystery seen in this world is part of the one mystery of the world.

S: We were conceiving of Prajāpati serially as the year, the month, the day, in terms of time. Abruptly we turn here to think of Prajāpati as food, a material entity. How is this sudden leap justified?

G: We have a sense of time only because there are events. Do you know that?

S: That is true. No events, no time!

G: And there can be no events unless there are material entities. An event is the phenomenon of one state of existence changing to another. What we call birth is but the emergence of a new state of existence. Now tell me, can we separate the turning of the wheel of time from the emergences of new forms?

S: No.

G: The birth of a new living being is the most dynamic and vital of all transformations.

S: Now I understand.

G: To visualise together the principle of couplehood, the wheel of time turning, the occurrence of transformations, the birth of a child — all of these as part of one picture of life is what makes any search of this kind fruitful. Trying to relate them logically makes no sense, for the simple reason that nature is not ruled by logic. Logic is something we have derived from nature's events; something of our making.

S: The food equated to Prajāpati here — is it the ordinary food we eat?

G: It is the ordinary food and something more at the same time. The food we eat gives us vitality and makes us virile. A cosmic food principle draws a link between our hunger, the growth of edibles in the world and the satisfaction of eating. This principle is none other than the principle of Prajāpati. The same principle materialises as sperm and ovum, which together become one in the newborn. It is now not necessary to treat the two as two, for the two together are now signified by the term *retas*. The duality of *prāṇa* and *rayī* also then becomes irrelevant.

तद् ये ह वै तत्प्रजापतिव्रतं चरन्ति ते मिथुनमुत्पादयन्ते।
तेषामेवैष ब्रह्मलोको येषां तपो ब्रह्मचर्यं येषु सत्यं प्रतिष्ठितम् ।। १५ ।।

tad ye ha vai tat prajāpati-vrataṁ caranti te mithunam utpādayante । *teṣām evaiṣa brahmaloko yeṣāṁ tapo brahmacaryaṁ yeṣu satyaṁ pratiṣṭhitam* ।। 15 ।।

Those who thus take the vow of Prajāpati beget couples. To them alone is given this world of Brahmā; theirs alone is *tapas* and *brahmacarya*; in them alone is Reality well-founded.

Seeker: Is this *prajāpati-vrata* a religious vow?

Guru: Many are the vows taken by devout people, but the present one is of a different order. Do you know what *vrata* means?

S: No.

G: It means, to do service in one pointed attention, with body, word and mind. To have a master-interest in life and to make these triple functions subservient to it are all implied in *vrata* (vow). Seeing Prajāpati, the all-inclusive creative principle, as pervading every pulsation of life is to be understood the *prajāpati-vrata* here. The usual religious vows need be observed only for a limited period of time; this is a vow to be kept for a whole life-time. The one aware of this Prajāpati principle, sees himself not merely as a being capable of begetting offspring, but also as a miniature replica of Prajāpati. What he does in the life will be that which is willed by Prajāpati, saying and thinking that which is willed by Prajāpati. It is thus that the *prajāpati vrata* becomes a natural thing, not self-imposed.

S: What is the implication of "They beget couples"?

G: It apparently means, they beget male and female children. Prajāpati, becoming desirous of offspring, produced a couple from himself, thinking they would produce all beings from them. So too man, the miniature Prajāpati, necessarily has to produce couples from himself so as to ensure continuity of life.

S: Prajāpati became desirous of offspring, did *tapas*, produced the couple, marking the beginning of the world. Do you mean that Prajāpati's function continues even now and will continue in future also?

G: The Prajāpati's story we saw at the beginning is a myth which symbolises that the process of creation has been going on incessantly and will continue for ever through all living beings.

S: It is said, "To them alone is given *Brahmaloka*". Is it the world attained through the northern path? Or is it an entirely differnt world?

G: Sperm and ovum were just seen as the worldly replica of *prāṇa* and *rayī*. Their union results in the formulation of the first cell of the new living being. It has to continue growing. The begetting of couple of this Stanza, in continuation of the stanza that indicated the formation of the first cell, has to be taken as implying the growth of the embryo, where the question of the duality of sperm and ovum, of *prāṇa* and *rayī*, and therefore of the northern path and the southern path, does not arise at all. One *prajāpati-vrata*, one principle of creation, alone functions there. Because of the creative urge, *karma*, inherent in *Brahman*, the creative process of growth goes on non-stop. Neither of the two paths leads to that awareness — only the path of awareness of *Brahman*, the all-creating Reality, can do that. Seeing that Reality in oneself, in one's creative potential, is the attainment of *Brahmaloka*.

S: That must be why it is said, 'In them alone is Reality well founded'.

G: Yes.

तेषामसौ विरजो ब्रह्मलोको न येषु जिह्ममनृतं न माया चेति ।। १६ ।।

teṣām asau virajo brahma-loko na yeṣu jihmam anṛtam
na māyā ceti ।। 16 ।।

To them is given that blameless world of Brahmā, in whom there is no crookedness, no falsehood, no trickery.

Guru: Concluding this chapter, this verse serves also as its *phalaśruti*.

Seeker: What is *phalaśruti*?

G: After elucidating an important teaching, it is usual in Indian scriptures, to state what the seeker will gain by its learning. This is called *phalaśruti*, *phala* meaning fruit or benefit, and *śruti* scriptural statement.

This chapter portrayed a vivid picture of *Brahman* with the natural process of procreation as its canvas, and concludes now with promising the attainment of *Brahmaloka* for those who take the vow of Prajāpati. *Tapas* and *brahmacarya* will naturally accompany such a vow. In those who have attained this goal alone is Reality well founded and living, as stated in the last stanza.

S: Does the absence of falsehood (*anṛtam*) mean the same state of Reality being well founded?

G: Basically the practices mentioned in these two stanzas are different in kind: those of the last stanza are studied ones, and of the present one natural expressions of one's inner awareness. The word *ṛtam* — *anṛtam* is its opposite — signifies the natural order of life as the self-expression of the creativity of *Brahman*.

S: How does the attainer become *viraja*?

G: Have you heard of the three *guṇas* of *prakṛti*, the modalities of nature?

S: Yes. They are *sattva-guṇa*, *rajo-guṇa* and *tamo-guṇa*.

G: What is characteristic of *rajo-guṇa*?

S: Those of *rajo-guṇa* are more active, and their motivation is personal benefit.

G: Will the one well-founded in Reality be motivated by any personal gain?

S: Not at all.

G: The state of remaining free from motivated activities is called *viraja*, literally the absence of *rajo-guṇa*. The word could also be construed as the absence of attachment (*rāga*). I-sense and mine-sense will be strong in those of *rajo-guṇa*. They will be fully absent in those who find themselves one with *Brahman*. Those who are free from attachments are known as *virāgis*, *viraja* a synonym of it.

S: Crookedness also will have no place naturally in the way of life of such a person. What is the *māyā* he does not have? It does not seem to be the *māyā* ordinarily understood in Vedānta.

G: *Māyā* has another sense here. Some, you must have noticed, have the habit of double dealing in their transactions. That is the *māyā* of this verse. A subtle psychological factor is implicit in this *māyā*.

S: What is it?

G: We always interact with others. Every action or reaction is an expression of or is motivated by some state of mind. Seeing such an action of one person, another reacts after making an evaluation of it, consciously or unconsciously. Such evaluations are always of what is externally seen in the other person and never of what is within him or her. It is almost impossible to evaluate fully the intention and state of mind of another person simply by observing what he does. To be more precise, a person need not necessarily be fully aware of what is really even within his own mind. A gap exists thus always between what is within one person and what is seen by another in him. The real personality of one person always remains unobserved by anyone else. The face one shows is thus a mask for another. Sometimes a person hides his intensions and shows a masked face to the world which in turn observes still another face, a third face, the basis of all reaction. Even the people observing these masked faces are themselves wearing masks of their own. Such is the world of *māyā* we are in. Those who make Reality their own home alone will be free of this *māyā*. Putting emphasis on this point the *Kena Upaniṣad* has in it a peculiar usage *satyam āyatanam*, meaning the state in which Reality is one's own proper home. One lives unmasked in his own home. Reality becoming ones own home makes one unmasked.

S: This is a new revelation to me. The final teaching, I have heard, of Vedānta is 'The knower of *Brahman* becomes *Brahman*.' How is it to be fitted into the Prajāpati concept of this chapter?

G: Prajāpati is *Brahman* understood in the context of creation. Procreating beings, every living being is a Prajāpati; every human being is a Prajāpati. The teaching of this chapter could be summarised thus: One who knows Prajāpati becomes Prajāpati.

Second Question

द्वितीयः प्रश्नः

**अथ हैनं भार्गवो वैदर्भिः पप्रच्छ। भगवन् कत्येव देवाः प्रजां विधारयन्ते?
कतर एतत्प्रकाशयन्ते? कः पुनरेषां वरिष्ठ इति ॥ १ ॥**

atha hainaṁ bhārgavo vaidarbhiḥ papraccha ।
bhagavan, katyeva devāḥ prajāṁ vidhārayante? katara
etat prakāśayante? kaḥ punar eṣāṁ variṣṭha iti ॥ 1 ॥

Then Bhārgava of Vidarbha asked Pippalāda: Venerable Sir, how many *deva*s do sustain created beings? How many of them do make themselves manifest? And who again is the greatest among them?

Seeker: Bhārgava's question presupposes that *deva*s, the denizens of heaven, sustain this world. How to explain this presupposition?

Guru: We examined *deva*s as part of our study of the Peace Invocation. Each specific way in which consciousness finds expression is a *deva*, irrespective of whether such expressions are cosmic or individual; the present context being of the latter.

S: Why is it so?

G: The theme discussed in the last chapter ended with the begetting of children through the mating of male and female as part of an overall scheme of life. Now the question is the continuance of the newborn, as indicated by the first word of this chapter, *atha* (now then). Bhārgava's questions are about the factors that enable the born to endure. Yet he delimits the scope of his equiry after each question.

S: How?

G: First he asks about all the gods that sustain created beings. Then he asks, how many of them make themselves known by self-manifesting. Still further, he wants to know who is the greatest of them and this last question, you will find later, leads to further improvement on what we saw in the last chapter.

S: Kindly explain it.

G: From Prajāpati emerged *rayī* and *prāṇa*, *rayī* constituting the concrete and *prāṇa* that which is beyond concretisation. The same *prāṇa* in a profounder sense, not as one of the causal factors of creation, will be seen in this chapter as the greatest of all *devas* — the Supreme Self. Bhārgava's question thus leads to sublimating *prāṇa* to a new height.

S: Gods, as symbols of various functions of consciousness, are graded here. Are there such grades in the function of consciousness also?

G: Yes, there are. Even gross and inert entitites, like earth, as will be stated in the next stanza, are manifest forms of one and same consciousness. Its subtlest and noblest function is of knowing itself. Consciousness has thus inherent in it the power to manifest as a vast range of appearences constituting the world. Knowing the mysterious structure of the self-expression of consciousness itself is the knowing of the meaning of life. The *prāṇa* represented here as the greatest of all *devas*, leads us to that awareness.

तस्मै स होवाचाकाशो ह वा एष देवो वायुरग्निरापः पृथिवी वाङ्मनश्चक्षुः श्रोत्रं च। ते प्रकाश्याभिवदन्ति वयमेतद्बाणमवष्टभ्य विधारयामः।। २ ।।

tasmai sa hovāca ākāśo ha vā eṣa devo vāyur agnir āpaḥ pṛthivī vāṅ manaś cakṣuḥ śrotraṁ ca । *te prakāśyābhivadanti vayam etad bāṇam avaṣṭabhya vidhārayāmaḥ* ।। 2 ।।

To him, he (Pippalāda) said: Space verily is such a god, so too are wind, fire, water, earth, speech, mind, eye, ear. They, becoming illumined, declare: "We sustain this arrow in coherence".

Seeker: The five basic elements space, air, fire, water and earth are counted here as gods along with speech, mind, eyes and ears. Air, fire and water are Vedic gods and earth is a goddess, but space (*ākāśa*), as far as I know, is not a god. The senses too, as means of illumining knowledge, are often treated as gods. But the present ordering of gods conforms to none of these. It looks like a mess of many things. Could you please clarify how this ordering is to be understood?

Guru: This ordering of gods does not follow any prevailing order or system.

S: Then?

G: What is supposedly done by these gods?

S: They sustain each one of us.

G: All the factors — physical, biological, mental — together are represented as gods here. All gods are not enumerated in detail, some of representative character alone are mentioned.

S: We are sustained by the food we eat, the air we breath in, the water we take and the like. Are all these to be counted as gods?

G: There is a basic mistake in this sustainer-sustained concept.

S: How? Aren't we sustained by them?

G: All such factors are inseparably correlated. They constitute our being, yet they are not related to us as our sustainers.

S: Then?

G: The sustainer-sustained relationship involves two entities, one sustaining the other, both existing separately. No such separation is possible in the present case. Our existence and the existence of the factors mentioned here are inseparable. They do not *exist* separate; we *understand* them as separate. Our existence is simply one, but we understand it as constituted of many.

S: Do you mean that we are not constituted of many factors?

G: Yes, I do. Each one of us exists as a whole being. Our analytical mind, in its inquisitiveness, makes an imaginary separation of many factors, and then conceives the idea that our being is constituted of them. Separating and then putting together, both operations are imaginary; they do not and cannot take place in actual life. All our scientific enquiry has this imaginary separation and putting together for its basis — the basic mistake I told you about. In Vedānta this mistake is known as *avidyā* (ignorance). A mysterious mistake, it is also known as *māyā*. In short, to see our existence and the existence of the sustaining factors as separate is a basic error, the same is true with considering our existence as an aggregate of all of them.

S: Now it is somewhat clear to me. It is our mind that created all this separateness.

Space (*ākāśa*) as a god is treated separately here. Why is it so?

G: Space is the one entity that gives room for all else to exist, so it belongs to an order of its own. The Sanskrit word *ākāśa* itself literally means the same.

S: But mind and speech, we know, do not exist in space.

G: What you say is right when you think of a 'physical' space in which everything 'physical' exists. Now, where does the 'physical' space exist?

S: I have never thought of it. Where can the boundless space exist other than in our imagination!

G: You are right. It is in the space of consciousness, called *cidākāśa*, that even external space has its being. Our mental functions and speech also exist in that space. This space of consciousness will be seen in the coming chapter as the Self (*ātman*) the one Reality that unfolds itself as everything, as gods, as sustainer and sustained. These *deva*s do not therefore conform to any prevailing system of thought.

S: Everyone of these gods boasts of being the sustainer of 'this arrow'. Which is this 'this arrow'?

G: We are here concerned with the factors that sustain us and therefore each one of us is the arrow.

S: How can we think of ourselves as arrows?

G: Arrow is meant to be shot at a target. Only when an arrow hits its target, is its existence justified. So too, our existence is justified and becomes meaningful when it strikes at its final goal. Our life here is comparable to the flight of an arrow. In the absence of such a goal, life would be felt to stray purposelessly, a major problem the human race is facing at the moment. With no constant principal interest in life, one finds oneself entangled in changeful momentary interests, causing loss of stability. Monetary gain, though fleeting, is one value that enchants all and dominates other values. Each value dominating others at a particular moment is also allegorically implicit in gods claiming superiority over the others. The boasting of these gods is comparable to the feelings of a soldier who occupies a key position at the war front. Forgetting that he is only a minute part of a gigantic war-machinery, he thinks that without him the battle cannot be won. Actually he is unable to do anything other than perform his part in the war-moves. So too, each of the *devas*, though without any independent and separable function, thinks he controls the whole system.

S: Why are these gods so boastful?

G: The only apparent reason is attributing human boastfulness to gods. To be boastful is part of human life. Of no utility, boastfulness swells up one's egoism leading one to making hell of one's own life. Happy with themselves, those who are not boastful lead a peaceful life.

S: It might be to warn us of this pitfall that the *ṛṣi* of the Upaniṣad made Bhārgava ask such a question?

G: It could be presumed so. Anyway, Bhārgava's two questions have been answered in this stanza. The answer is given dramatically with the rivalry of the *devas* among themselves. The same mood continues in the next stanza also, where the stage is set for answering the third question.

तान् वरिष्ठः प्राण उवाच। मा मोहमापद्यथ अहमेवैतत्पञ्चधात्मानं प्रविभज्यैतद्बाणमवष्टभ्य विधारयामीति; तेऽश्रद्दधाना बभूवुः ।। ३ ।।

tān variṣṭhaḥ prāṇa uvāca । *mā moham āpadyatha aham evaitat pañcadhātmānaṁ pravibhajyaitad bāṇam avaṣṭabhya vidhārayāmi iti; te'śraddadhānā babhūvuḥ*
।। 3 ।।

> To them *prāṇa* the chief said: Do not be deluded; I alone, dividing myself five-fold, sustain this arrow. But they became faithless in him.

Seeker: *Prāṇa* who now speaks to the other gods was not seen among the gods mentioned just now. Isn't *prāṇa* a god?

Guru: *Prāṇa* was not mentioned among the gods, but here he appears as the chief of gods. It shows, he is not an ordinary god to be counted among others. As we proceed we'll see, in this chapter itself, *prāṇa* as the god who sustains all other gods, as the God of gods.

S: The word *prāṇa* is used here in a sense evidently different from the one in the last chapter. What is really meant by the word?

G: It is a word used in may Upaniṣads with varying nuances. The root *prāṇ* means to breathe, to respire, to inhale air. *Prāṇa* is thus the vital function that keeps a being alive, through respiration. The last chatper used the word in a sense very close to its etymological meaning. Its connotation in the present context we are just going to see in the coming stanzas.

S: What is the *moha* (delusion) that *prāṇa* warns of?

G: *Moha* is the delusion in which, not knowing what is real, one is misled to take the unreal as real. It happens more to us human beings than to the gods and hence *prāṇa*'s warning is for us also. We too, like the gods here, become proud of our capabilities. Sometimes we ask others, "Do you know what good things I have done for the world"?, completely oblivious of the reality that none of our capabilities is of our making; as we are part of nature, so our capabilities are also part of nature. It is nature that functions in the form of our existence, in the form of our activities. Even our free will and sense of responsibility are part of nature.

S: What are the five into which *prāṇa* divided himself?

G: A subject to be dealt with in detail in the next chapter, it need not be discussed here.

S: Is the faithlessness of gods in *prāṇa*'s words the opposite of *śraddhā* we saw in Chapter I?

G: Yes, it is. *Prāṇa*, while being the most vital life-sustaining principle, is also a symbol of the all knowing *Guru*. All the gods, boastful of their capabilities, are ignorant like us. We also, on being shown our real incapability by a *Guru*, will only ridicule him at first, as done by the gods here.

S: Many gods were seen as important in the last verse, whereas *prāṇa* alone is the chief god here. Which is true, the oneness of God or multiplicity of gods?

G: Multiplicity of gods is a Vedic concept and oneness of God is Vedāntic. The method of teaching generally adopted by Upaniṣads, with their Vedic background, while asserting the oneness of Reality, does not do away with the idea of multiplicity of gods. Even as gods are superseded by *prāṇa* in this context, the multiplicity of gods is superseded, not discarded, by the oneness of *Brahman*.

S: Vedānta, as I understood, is more concerned with *Brahman* than with God. How could we say it stands for oneness of God?

G: The theological God seated in heaven, it is true, is different from *Brahman*. But to an Indian mind, not prone to contrast with the theological God, both are the same. In the present case, the frame of reference of the present chapter demands such a concept. Neither the gods mentioned here are to be taken as Vedic gods, nor *prāṇa* as mere respiratory function; the latter is going to be sublimated and represented as *Brahman*.

S: The world, according to the last verse, is sustained by various gods, whereas *prāṇa* is seen here as the one chief god. Could we then conceive *prāṇa* as the aggregate function of all the gods?

G: No. Suppose a poet puts before you at random all the words of a poem. You will not be able to make the poem out of them. So too, the function of all the gods put together will not make *prāṇa*. One who is familiar with the poem knows which word comes where; he can shape the words into the poem. Likewise, on visualising the function of *prāṇa*, one will be able to find the place of each god in the total scheme of life.

सोऽभिमानादूर्ध्वमुत्क्रमत इव; तस्मिनुत्क्रामत्यथेतरे सर्वं एवोत्क्रामन्ते, तस्मिँश्च प्रतिष्ठमाने सर्व एव प्रातिष्ठन्ते। तद्यथा मक्षिका मधुकरराजानमुत्क्रामन्तं

सर्वा एवोत्क्रामन्ते, तस्मिंश्च प्रतिष्ठमाने सर्वा एव प्रातिष्ठन्त, एवं वाङ्मनश्चक्षुः श्रोत्रं च ते प्रीताः प्राणं स्तुन्वन्ति ॥ ४ ॥

so'bhimānād ūrdhvam utkramata iva; tasmin utkrāmaty athetare sarva evotkrāmante, tasmiṁś ca pratiṣṭhamāne sarva eva prātiṣṭhante । tad yathā makṣikā madhu-kara-rājānam utkrāmantaṁ sarvā evotkrāmante, tasmiṁś ca pratiṣṭhamāne sarvā eva prātiṣṭhanta, evaṁ vāṅ manaś cakṣuḥ śrotraṁ ca te prītāḥ prāṇaṁ stunvanti ॥ 4 ॥

He from indignation pretended to rise up (from the body). At his rising up all other (gods) were also found rising up. On his settling down they were also found settling down.

On the queen bee's rising up all bees rise up, and all settle down when the queen bee settles down. Even so are speech, mind, sight, hearing and so on. Satisfied, they praise *prāṇa* thus:

Seeker: As *prāṇa* was supposed to be superior, his indignation and pride do not suit him, the symbol of wisdom.

Guru: Your doubt is pertinent. We are only at the second stage of developing *Brahma-vidyā* with a well conceived method. The wisdom represented by *prāṇa* is therefore not mature enough to be rid of the pride of being superior, another characteristic of human beings. Though eventually going to be glorified by the other gods as *Brahman* itself, *prāṇa* has not yet attained that glory as could be presumed from the question with which the next chapter begins, namely, "Whence is this *prāṇa* born?"

S: Don't these gods, symbols of senses, mind and so on, know of their dependence on *prāṇa*?

G: They do. This is simply a dramatic situation created by the *ṛṣi* to teach us human beings an important lesson.

S: What is it?

G: That when life goes on unhindered no one cares to knowing how it works. But, when things go wrong, people worry, and make them ponder on the meaning of their plans for life, and of the meaning of life itself. This human characteristic is dramtically presented here in the guise of gods' predicament. First they were boastful, then they became submissive and finally began to glorify *prāṇa*.

S: Comparing gods to bees seems to be a very meaningful allegory.

G: Yes. The Upaniṣadic *ṛṣis* are poets. Their allegorical allusions make the comprehension of philosophical vision easier and sweeter. When *prāṇa* ceases functioning, all other faculties also cease to function; the person becomes dead. *Prāṇa*'s function as separate is relevant only because we started with treating each faculty as a god. No such question of superiority or inferiority arises on seeing the organic function of a living being as one whole. The superiority of *prāṇa* is therefore meaningful only in a limited field of vision.

एषोऽग्निस्तपत्येष सूर्य एष पर्जन्यो मघवानेष वायुः ।
एष पृथिवी रयिर्देवः सदसच्चामृतं च यत् ।। ५ ।।

eṣo'gnis tapaty eṣa sūrya eṣa parjanyo maghavān eṣa vāyuḥ । *eṣa pṛthivī rayir devaḥ sad-asac cāmṛtaṁ ca yat* ।। 5 ।।

As fire He burns; He is the sun; He is rain as well as rain-god (Maghavān); He is the wind; He is the earth, *rayī* and gods. He is being and non-being and the Immortal too.

Guru: To appreciate fully the significance of this exaltation you have to see how the various factors or elements equated to *prāṇa* are interrelated.

Seeker: Kindly clarify.

G: The gods are drawing an integrated overall picture of *prāṇa* that unfolds itself as everything from fire to the Immortal. The two entities first contrasted are fire and the sun, both hot and with the quality of heating, the former of worldly existence and the latter other-worldly as conceived by the poetic imagery of the Upaniṣad. Sometimes fire is treated as effect and the sun its cause in an allegorical sense. Both cause and effect, the worldly and the other-worldly, are but emanations from the same *prāṇa*. Rain and Maghavān are also related likewise. Rain the earthly effect and Maghavān (Indra), as rain-god, its other-worldly cause.

S: Wind and earth, it seems, unlike the two previous pairs, stand for the five basic physical elements. Am I right?

G: Yes, you are. Of the five basic elements, space provides room for the others to exist, wind being the subtlest of them and earth the grossest. Wind and earth together stand for the physical world.

S: Why is *rayī* brought in again?

G: *Prāṇa* and *rayī* were the primal twins that emerged from Prajāpati. Here, in the present chapter, *prāṇa* is sublimated as the source of everything, equal to Prajāpati. Bringing back *rayī* here suggests that both the *prāṇa* and *rayī* of the last chapter are to be conceived as manifestations of the *prāṇa* of this chapter.

S: *Prāṇa*, the source of all, as *sat*, the substance underlying everything, is understandable. How could it be treated as *sat* and *asat* (being and non-being) at once?

G: It is one of the paradoxes that bring in philosophy. There would have been no phiolosophy were there no paradox in life. Paradoxes and their transcendence is the crux of philosophy and that is why often at the heart of Upaniṣadic teachings there appears a paradox.

The idea of 'being' presupposes that of 'non-being'; without one the other is meaningless. Both ideas emerge in consciousness. Our experience of a thing can be either of its existence or its non-existence; either way it is an experience. The original words for 'being' and 'non-being' are *sat* and *asat*. *Sat* in Vedāntic parlance means that which exists with no temporal or spatial limitations. *Asat* does not mean absolute non-existence, but that which appears to be real, yet is not real by itself, like the appearance of waves in the ocean or water in a mirage. The two terms are equivalent to the 'reality' and 'appearance' in Western philosophy. Ocean and waves, though *conceived* as two, do not *exist* as two in actuality. Put otherwise, a non-dual reality when looked at from one point of view, appears as ocean and from another point of view it appears as waves. These different views and appearances do not in any way affect the oneness of what really exists. So too, the concepts of *sat* and *asat* are understood to emerge from the non-dual *prāṇa*. As beginning and end are relevant only with appearances, *prāṇa* is without beginning and end, birth or death, and thus it is immortal (*amṛta*).

S: Can't we consider all, from fire to the immortal, as effect and *prāṇa* as cause?

G: Yes, we can, but with the clear awareness that our ultimate aim is transcending the duality of cause and effect, rather than discerning which is cause and which is effect. To visualise cause as assuming the form of all effects means to see cause and effect as inseparable. Western thought, following the tradition of Plato, prefers to consider cause as of the world of 'intelligibles' and effect as of 'visibles'. Though the Indian equivalent to 'intelligibles' is *cintyam*, Indian thinkers do not consider the causal reality as 'intelligible', but as its opposite *acintyam* in the sense 'inconceivable'.

S: Why is this dispsarity?

G: The Indian concepts of the visible (*dṛśyam*), does not exclude the mentally conceivable which is equivalent to the Platonic 'intelligible'. The centre of a huge fly-wheel in motion is an invisible, minute, motionless point. In the like manner, that which sustains all apparent and constantly changing forms, including cause and effect, is invisible and inconceivably subtle, subject to no change. The *ṛṣi*'s of India therefore prefer to designate it as 'the inconceivable', 'the ineffable', even 'the unnameable'. The next stanza makes use of the very same analogy of the wheel and its centre to clarify this point.

अरा इव रथनाभौ प्राणे सर्वं प्रतिष्ठितम् ।
ऋचो यजूँषि सामानि यज्ञः क्षत्रं ब्रह्म च ॥ ६ ॥

arā iva ratha-nābhau prāṇe sarvaṁ pratiṣṭhitam ।
ṛco yajūṁṣi sāmāni yajñaḥ kṣatraṁ brahma ca ॥ 6 ॥

Like spokes in the hub of a wheel, all are well fixed in *prāṇa* — the *Ṛg* (verses) the *Yajuṣ* (formulas) and the *Sāman* (chants), as also sacrifice, valour and wisdom.

Seeker: The same idea of the last verse, it seems, is presented here with the help of the wheel analogy.

Guru: Yes, it is the same idea, but a reversal of approach should not be missed.

S: What is the reversal?

G: That everything apparent emerges from one *prāṇa*, the unfolding of one into many, was pictured in the last stanza. The theme of this verse is, many remaining well fixed in the one. Going out from the centre of the wheel to the periphery was the approach of the last verse, whereas going into the centre from the periphery is the way of the present one.

S: Is there any particular reason for this reversal?

G: Yes, there is. Non-dual awareness is the ultimate goal of this enquiry. This awareness is neither of the 'many' unfolded from the 'one' nor of the central 'one' in which the 'many' are well-fixed, it is rather of the One Reality in which the centre and the periphery, the one and the many, are inseparable, as is to be seen in the next stanza. What remains after the mutual cancellation of the two opposing approaches is the non-dual One, not covered by the meaning of either of the verses.

S: Why can't that be presented directly, instead of resorting to this roundabout way?

G: With the limitations of our reasoning mind and language, which are incapable of grasping and expressing this non-dual Reality, the reasoning mind divides the Real into 'reality' and 'appearance', the one and the many and into many such pairs of opposites. Then we attempt to logically relate the one with the many and find it impossible. Only language, and no other means, is at our disposal. Language is incapable of helping us to express the non-dual, which remains unaffected by any imaginary division. The *ṛṣi*s of India devised an unusual, meta-logical method of expressing it: to present two opposing approaches side by side, leaving the seeker to search the non-dual out meditatively. Negating the forwardness of thought from the one and the backwardness of thought form the other, what remains as a residue of the inner content of both the statements will be the non-dual.

Sometimes explicitly stated, at other times implicit as in the present case, this method had been used by *ṛṣis* since the very ancient past. Such passages as, "One who knows *vidyā* and *avidyā* together" of the *Īśa Upaniṣad*(9); "Non-being has no becoming and being is not without becoming; the conclusion in regard to what is within these two has been known to true philosophers" of the *Bhagavad Gītā* (II.16) doubtlessly suggest such a method of approach that transcends the limitations of logical thinking and verbal expression. Called *yoga buddhi* by the *Bhagavad Gītā*, this method was known to Plato as 'dialectics' and he qualified it as 'the coping stone of widsom'. It is the same method that we tried to elucidate earlier with the help of the gold and ornament analogy. The non-dual Real is where the eternal gold and the transient ornament remain inseparable.

S: I think it is somewhat clear to me, yet I know it is not something to be *understood*; it is to be intuitively *perceived* in meditation.

Why is there a special reference to the Vedas, *yajña*, *kṣatram* and *brahman* as well fixed in *prāṇa*?

G: The special place of the *Atharvaveda* to which the present Upaniṣad is appended, had been noticed by us while examining the Peace Invocation. This Upaniṣad, in this particular context, conceives *prāṇa* as the Absolute Reality, and, given the superiority of the *Atharvaveda* in the wisdom context, the other Vedas are, with a certain element of exaggeration, conceived as well fixed in *prāṇa*, the Absolute.

S: All the Vedas, we know, are sublime wisdom variously expressed. Couldn't we consider then that the *prāṇa* of this context represents unconditioned Consciousness, *cit*, and the other three Vedas represent its own variegated manifest forms?

G: Yes, we can. In fact it is not merely a possibility, but rather is meant to be interpreted that way. All branches of knowledge, mundane and spiritual, could also be then seen as rooted in *prāṇa*. All sciences, all branches of human pursuit, we know, are nothing but expressions of different functional modes of one and the same consciousness with various value notions. With the word *sarvam* (all or everything) which covers this aspect also, usually we forget to include the vast mental world, as extensive as the physical world. This shortcoming of the human mind is made good by including the Vedas also within the scope of the word *sarvam* (all).

S: Why is *yajña*, Vedic sacrifice, specially mentioned as fixed in *prāṇa*?

G: *Yajña* as a philosophical concept has been examined by us while going through the Peace Invocation. As a Vedic ritual, it is motivated by some desire, an inner urge of a man's mind. This urge is fulfilled only when the inner urge of the cosmic mind agrees with it. All *yajña*s therefore have implicit in them a prayer for the harmony of the inner urges of the cosmic mind and individual minds. The individual performing the *yajña*, the gods who are meant to be made benevolent, the actual performance, the things offered, the burning of the fire — all these are elements that express the aspiration for the harmony of these two inner urges. It becomes actualised only as willed by the Absolute, and thus is well fixed in *prāṇa*.

S: Is it to be understood that the entire world revolves with the unmoving *prāṇa* for its centre, like a wheel rotating around an unmoving centre?

G: Such an envisioning is not to be ruled out. Though appearing motionless, the centre of a wheel is highly active. So too is the *prāṇa*. Its activity is not visible to our eyes, yet is the dynamic force central to all the rotating movements of the world both physical and mental. *Prāṇa* as understood here is the urge that invisibly causes everything to be in a state of constant flux.

> **प्रजापतिश्चरसि गर्भे त्वमेव प्रतिजायसे। तुभ्यं प्राण प्रजास्त्विमा बलिं हरन्ति य: प्राणै: प्रतितिष्ठसि ।। ७ ।।**
>
> *prajāpatiścarasi garbhe tvam eva pratijāyase । tubhyaṁ prāṇa prajāstvimā baliṁ haranti yaḥ prāṇaiḥ pratitiṣṭhasi* ।। 7 ।।
>
> O *Prāṇa*, as Prajāpati you move within wombs; you yourself are born repeatedly. These creatures, in each of whom you dwell along with *prāṇa*s, bring offerings to you.

Seeker: Is the *prāṇa* moving within wombs as Prajāpati similar to the burning of fire and the shining of the sun spoken of Stanza 5?

Guru: So it looks at first glance, but an apparent change in the mood of the gods who glorify *prāṇa* is not to be missed.

S: How is their mood changed?

G: In the last two stanzas the gods referred to *prāṇa* as 'he' (*eṣaḥ*) in the third person. Now they address *prāṇa* directly as 'you' in the second person, presumably due to an emotional change brought about by the two previous verses. The gods appear to have established a sort of intimacy with *prāṇa*, transcending intellectual understanding. We, the seekers, are also therefore required to comprehend this stanza with an emotional leaning if we are to do justice to it. Finding oneself an inseparable ripple of the ocean of *prāṇa*'s creative urge, seeing one's nothingness in that ocean, one feels an emotional ardour towards *prāṇa*.

S: The words, "Yourself are born repeatedly" resound with the idea of reincarnation of souls.

G: Certain ideas getting fixed in the mind conditioning it, and colouring other ideas, is a peculiarity and weakness of human nature. The reincarnation of souls is one such idea deeply rooted in the Indian minds. But in the search for Relaity, it is the clear insight of *ṛṣis*, and not any preconceived idea of our own, that is to be our guide. The *prāṇa* understood here is, we know, *Brahman* itself in a permanently active, creative state, never inert. The creative urge in it results in the continuous appearance of its own manifest forms along with the disappearance of the old, of which former we call birth and the latter death. Birth and death are two facets of the creative self-expression of the one and only Reality. It is in and through these beginningless and endless births and deaths of manifest forms that one Reality endures indestructible. *Prāṇa* as Prajāpati, assuming all the constantly changing forms himself, is considered as born again and again: "Yourself are born repeatedly."

S: How do all the creatures carry offerings to *prāṇa*?

G: Gods are in a supplicant mood here. As they pay homage to *prāṇa*, they feel the whole world pays homage. A deeper implicit significance is also to be noticed in this offering.

S: What is it?

G: How do all creatures muster enough vitality to keep alive, to function consciously?

S: That vitality is in all of us as part of the creative vitality of nature.

G: It is that total vitality of nature which is conceived here as *prāṇa*. Realising that acting and reacting, physically, mentally and verbally, is but the creative self-expression of the one and only *prāṇa*, one begins to see all one's activities as nature's action and therefore not one's own. In our ignorance, we consider the activities performed by us as 'our actions'. On becoming aware of the one creative Reality and its actions, one becomes inclined to offer back to nature all actions mistaken as one's own. All religious offerings and rituals, symbolise this awareness and giving back, and is the origin of the *yajña* concept as we have already seen.

S: How does *prāṇa* dwell in creatures along with *prāṇas*?

G: The reference to many *prāṇas* here is anticipative of what we are going to learn in the next chapter where all the different *prāṇas* will be discussed in detail.

> देवानामसि वह्नितमः पितॄणां प्रथमा स्वधा ।
> ऋषीणां चरितं सत्यमथर्वाङ्गिरसामसि ॥ ८ ॥

> *devānām asi vahnitamaḥ pitṝṇāṁ prathamā svadhā* ।
> *ṛṣīṇāṁ caritaṁ satyam atharvāṅgirasām asi* ॥ 8 ॥

> Among gods you are the best carrier (of offerings). Among manes you are the first *svadhā* offering. Of *ṛṣi*s like Atharvān and Aṅgiras you are their truthful conducts.

Seeker: What is the significance of seeing certain items of high value alone as *prāṇa*?

Guru: The *prāṇa* of this chapter was first seen as chief among gods, as the basic vital function that keeps all other functions alive, and finally *prāṇa* was seen as *Brahman* itself, whose apparent but unreal forms constitute this world. The rest of the chapter, from this stanza onwards, has a semblance of the *vibhūti yoga* of the *Bhagavad Gītā*, where the best among the manifestations of the Absolute, of various grades and values, are pointed out as the Absolute itself. It is not merely an account of the various beings and entities as such, but a tabling of their value.

S: It is the gods who praise *prāṇa*. How can they see one among them an equal to *prāṇa*?

G: Gods as seen in this chapter, emerge, live and move as ordained by *prāṇa*. Among the gods it is Fire who has been assigned the special status of the carrier of offerings from the world of men to the world of Vedic gods: *Vahni*, another name for fire, literally means 'the carrier' and *Vahnitama* means the best carrier. Fire as the god who links men and gods together is equated to *prāṇa*, the God of gods, who keeps united all the gods.

S: Who are *pitṛ*s?

G: Another tradition of India holds that the souls of the ancestors, called *pitṛ*s, are to be propitiated by human beings for a happy life here on earth. Pre-Vedic in origin, this concept was later absorbed into the Vedic tradition.

S: Is *svadhā* one among the *pitṛ*s?

G: The ancestors of the worshipper, *pitṛ*s have never been named individually. *Svadhā* is the most important ritual offering made to the manes. It consists of balls of cooked rice, also called *piṇḍa*. Such offerings are always accompanied by the uttering of sacred words called *mantras*. Traditionally, the sacred words uttered along with offerings made to the gods (*devas*) have necessarily to end with the word *svāhā* and those meant for the manes with *svadhā*. Thus in the actual offering made, *svadhā* is the rice ball (*piṇḍa*), and among the sacred words, it is the word uttered last along with every offering.

S: These are all meaningful as rituals, but how are they relevant here in the wisdom context?

G: The two paths, of the gods and manes, or any other path, can exist and function only in and with the vitality derived from *prāṇa*, thus meaningful in the wisdom context also.

S: How is the truthful conduct of a *ṛṣi* equal to *prāṇa*?

G: The word *ṛṣi* means a seer, the seer of Reality. His way of living and behaviour will naturally be in line with Reality. Reality is not merely *understood* by him, but lived and practised by him. *Ṛṣis* are the real practisers of Reality, the embodiments of Reality, and Reality living.

S: Why are Atharvān and Aṅgiras considered as ideal *ṛṣis*?

G: Both of them belong to the *Atharva* tradition of the Vedas, the tradition of the present Upaniṣad. All the Vedas are the recorded utterings of *ṛṣis*; they gain strength as scriptures from their wisdom content, which mainly is rooted in the *Atharvaveda*. One *prāṇa*, pure Consciousness in essence, assumes the form of the ideas, words, scriptures and their wisdom teaching. Such an insight is behind conceiving Atharvān and Aṅgiras and their way of life as *prāṇa*.

S: Is there a set of beings called *devas* (gods)?

G: Some believe so and some do not. Neither has any supporting evidence and therefore both will ever remain beliefs.

S: What is the relevance of such a belief?

G: Our modern science, as you know, categorises everything in this world into three kingdoms; the mineral kingdom, the vegetable kingdom, the animal kingdom. Man is placed at the topmost rung of the last one. If at all minerals are conscious, do you think they will know and appreciate the nature of existence of vegetables and animals?

S: Not at all.

G: Likewise is the inability of those in the vegetable kingdom to understand and appreciate animal life. Understanding the nature of human life, similarly, is impossible for other animals. Similarly, if at all there is life above that of humans, it would be beyond the comprehension of human beings. By denying the possibility of such a life, in essence, we'll be making our incapability the criterion in asserting or denying the existence of something. May be there is such a realm of life, may be not. Our *ṛṣis* in their poetical elation describe many worlds above the human world. To downgrade them as meaningless is equal to giving up poetry.

S: Has the word *aṅgi* anything to do with the name Aṅgiras of the *ṛṣi*?

G: Possibly there is. *Aṅgi* means that which has parts (*aṅga*), *rasa* means 'essence' or 'essential value'. Aṅgiras thus means 'the essential content or value of the one who possesses parts'.

S: What are the *aṅga*s or limbs then?

G: The context being that of contrasting Vedic traditions, the Atharva tradition, in which wisdom dominates, could be considered as the one with *aṅga*s (limbs) and the other three Vedas as limbs. Even as *prāṇa* is the essential content of the functions of all the senses as well as of that which is sensed, so the *ṛṣi*s of the Atharva tradition, with their conduct of life fully true to wisdom, represent the essential content and value of all the Vedic traditions.

इन्द्रस्त्वं प्राण तेजसा रुद्रोऽसि परिरक्षिता ।
त्वमन्तरिक्षे चरसि सूर्यस्त्वं ज्योतिषां पतिः ॥ ९ ॥

indras tvaṁ prāṇa tejasā rudro'si parirakṣitā ।
tvam antarikṣe carasi sūryas tvaṁ jyotiṣāṁ patiḥ ॥ 9 ॥

O Prāṇa, you are Indra by your valour; you are Rudra the protector; you are the sun orbiting in the atmosphere, the lord of the luminaries.

Seeker: How are Indra, Rudra and Sūrya (the sun) excellent manifest forms of *prāṇa*?

Guru: Indra, Rudra and Sūrya are Vedic gods, yet their functions are in different worlds. Indra is the chief of the gods, the denizens of heaven (*svarga*), the world above. Indra's displacement will result in the displacement of all the gods, similar to the perishing of the senses at the uprooting of *prāṇa* in the human body. All this takes place in the upper world, whereas the sun orbits in the middle region called *antarikṣa*, protecting the world below. Indra and Sūrya could thus be taken as representing the vital principles that sustain the higher world and the world here. Rudra also protects this world, not by diffusing energy but by protecting beings from negative forces, as the name itself connotes: one who makes cruel forces weep. *Prāṇa* appearing as these three gods of the three worlds, suggests that all the different worlds have only one sustaining Reality.

S: The epithet 'Lord of the luminaries' does not seem to fit in with the gods mentioned.

G: You are right in one sense, but in another sense it refers to a general characteristic of all the gods.

S: How is it?

G: The Sanskrit word for god is *deva*, literally 'brightness in essence'. *Jyotis* is another word for brightness. To be brightness in essence is common with all gods. Lord of the luminaries thus stands for the God of gods, the one who endows godhood to all the gods.

S: The sun in our ordinary experience is the chief of heavenly luminaries like stars and planets. Is this sense to be ignored?

G: Not at all, it actually adds beauty to the metaphysical principle represented.

> यदा त्वमभिवर्षस्यथेमाः प्राण ते प्रजाः ।
> आनन्दरूपास्तिष्ठन्ति कामायान्नं भविष्यतीति ।। १० ।।

> *yadā tvaṁ abhivarṣasy athemāḥ prāṇa te prajāḥ* ।
> *ānanda-rūpās tiṣṭhanti kāmāyānnaṁ bhaviṣyatīti* ।। 10 ।।

O Prāṇa, these creatures of yours live as embodiments of happiness on seeing you pouring down as rain, thinking of the possibility of sufficient food.

Seeker: What is the significance of seeing *prāṇa* in the form of rain?

Guru: We have been seeing *prāṇa* from Stanza 8 onwards as various life sustaining principles, significantly water, as the rule is, "no water, no life". The sun sustains life by diffusing energy from above whereas when water pours down, materially life is sustained as if from below.

S: Always thinking of food, all creatures, it seems, are concerned with material values only.

G: The structuring of life is such that it is sustained by food. Food is therefore, not merely a material value, it is a life-sustaining value. The Upaniṣads in fact do not make a clear division of material and spiritual values. Instead they grade life values hierarchically ranging from food (*annam*) to happiness (*ānandam*). Food is the most earthly value and happiness or absolute freedom the highest. All other values of life have their respective places in between these two extremes. Life at its grossest level is sustained by food for which water is a must. Subtlity and grossness are two extreme facets of our existence, whose corresponding values are freedom and food. And all these are self-expressions of the one Absolute Reality or *prāṇa*. What do you feel on eating when hungry?

S: I feel satisfied.

G: That satisfaction by itself — is it material or spiritual?

S: Food we know is material. When it becomes part of our body, again material; it results in the experiencing of happiness, a purely spiritual value. I don't see any boundary between material and spiritual here.

G: Food is to be perceived from an entirely different perspective in this context. The physical body is the grossest aspect of our existence, and happiness the subtlest and sublimest. The two are linked by food. If there is no water there can be no happiness of existing; if there is no *prāṇa* there is no function of senses.

S: To be the embodiment of Happiness is the final attainment. Here it says all creatures live as embodiments of happiness on seeing rain.

G: Such an inconsistency is revealed as we look at the situation, separating the existential (*sat*) aspect from the happiness (*ānanda*) aspect. The Real (*sat*) is Consciousness (*cit*), which unfolds and transforms itself as everything, actualising the Happiness (*ānanda*) content of itself; its outcome is the emergence of all beings, including food. Happiness always remains as the link between food and creatures. Creatures, seeing rain, hope for sufficient food; this is a part of this functional system. To hope for something means to be filled with the possibility of actualising happiness. *Prāṇa* is always charged with this inner urge for happiness and at every instance of relishing food this charge gets released in creatures. The *ānanda* content of our being and the relishing of food are thus inseparable.

व्रात्यस्त्वं प्राणैकऋषिरत्ता विश्वस्य सत्पतिः ।
वयमाद्यस्य दातारः पिता त्वं मातरिश्व नः ।। ११ ।।

vrātyas tvaṁ prāṇaika ṛṣir attā viśvasya satpatiḥ ।
vayam ādyasya dātāraḥ, pitā tvaṁ mātariśva naḥ ॥ 11 ॥

Untouched by initiatory rites, O Prāṇa, you are the one seer, the enjoyer, the Lord of all existences. O Mātariśvan, you are our father, we the givers of enjoyables.

Seeker: The epithet *vrātya*, meaning the one untouched by initiatory rites, used for *prāṇa* appears a little strange.

Guru: *Vrātya* is a word of reproval popular among ritualists, used for those who defy the ritualistic customs, a defiance that forms an essential prerequisite for attaining wisdom. According to the ancient ritualistic tradition, a human has to pass through sixteen purificatory rites, beginning with fertilisation rites and ending with funeral rites. Born free, every person, after undergoing each of these ceremonies, is bound in stages by the prevailing religious and social customs and at each stage losing a certain aspect of his freedom, until he becomes a non-entity indicated by the funeral rites. Ironically these ceremonies are supposed to be *saṁskāra vidhi*s, rites meant for making one more cultured ! Only a person bold enough to ignore all these rites and be free of their hold can hope to be a *jñānin* which is why he has to be untouched by initiatory rites. *Prāṇa* who represents the plenitude of wisdom, is thus so conceived. The best of such attainers of wisdom are known as *ṛṣi*s, the seers. The seers see Reality in themselves; a seer is therefore not merely a seer, but is the very Reality seen. Reality is one; *ṛṣi* in principle is also one only, *ekarṣi*. That one *ṛṣi*, none other than *Brahman*, is equated to *prāṇa*.

S: What does *prāṇa* eat and enjoy to call him *attā*?

G: Who is calling him so?

S: *Deva*s or senses.

G: What do the senses do as their natural function?

S: They are instrumental in the enjoyment of objects.

G: Are these senses on their own, capable of functioning so?

S: No. The senses function only when *prāṇa* keeps them alive.

G: Who is then the real enjoyer of objects?

S: *Prāṇa*, we must say.

G: The senses therefore tell *prāṇa*, "O Prāṇa, though grasped by us, the objects are really enjoyed by you".

Calling *prāṇa* the enjoyer suggests also the *ānanda* content of *Brahman*. As Vedānta teaches, happiness and suffering are the polarized forms in which the *ānanda* content of oneself becomes manifest.

S: How is *prāṇa* to be understood as *viśvasya satpatiḥ*?

G: It means the lord of all existences. *Brahman*, you know, is as much *sat* and *cit* as it is *ānanda*. As happiness and suffering are the manifest forms of the *ānanda* content of oneself, so too being and non-being of entities, are the manifest forms of *sat*. Likewise all knowledge, right or wrong, is the self-expression of the *cit*.

S: What enjoyables are given by senses? To whom are they given?

G: *Prāṇa* alone, as already seen, is the real enjoyer of everything. Yet *prāṇa* cannot enjoy unless there are objects made available by the senses. Thus there is a mutuality between *prāṇa* and the senses; this dialectical relationship renders one meaningless without the other. Where *prāṇa* is the enjoyer the senses provide the enjoyables. When *prāṇa* is all supporting as the functional basis, senses are the supported. It is therefore that the *deva*s consider *prāṇa* their father also.

S: Why is *prāṇa* praised as Mātariśvan?

G: Another name of air (Vāyu), Mātariśvān means one who moves within the womb of one's own mother. Air exists and moves, within space, its mother.

S: How does this aspect of air gain predominance here?

G: Air is the element that reaches everywhere. The discussion in this chapter moves around *prāṇa* whose basic function is breathing. Without air *prāṇa* has no function in any living being. Even as *prāṇa* moves within an individual being, so too Mātariśvān moves around within the cosmic being. The two are but two functional facets of one non-dual life-principle.

S: So far this chapter has been treating *prāṇa* as *Brahman*. Why is its sense shifted here towards individual beings?

G: This is the last of the present series of verses glorifying *prāṇa*, which at the beginning of the chapter was seen as the vitality that sustains all basic functional factors in an individual. *Prāṇa* was then sublimated and seen as *Brahman*. Before concluding the chapter *prāṇa* is again seen as related to individual beings and is asked in the next stanza not to leave this body. Calling it *prāṇa* and Mātariśvān together in this verse prepares the ground for a descent from the cosmic to the individual. The next two concluding stanzas see *prāṇa* in a purely individuated sense.

या ते तनूर्वाचि प्रतिष्ठिता या श्रोत्रे या च चक्षुषि ।
या च मनसि सन्तता शिवां तां कुरु मोत्क्रमीः ।। १२ ।।

yā te tanūr vāci pratiṣṭhitā yā śrotre yā ca cakṣuṣi ।
yā ca manasi santatā śivāṁ tāṁ kuru motkramīḥ ।। 12 ।।

That subtle form of yours, the firm basis of speech, ears and eyes, which pervades mind too incessantly, please make it auspicious; do not depart.

Seeker: *Prāṇa* is again seen, it seems, like at the beginning of this chapter, as the basis of all the senses.

Guru: Yes, the perspective is almost similar. The word *tanu* means 'physical body' as well as 'the subtle'. This subtle *prāṇa* was not visible to the gods and they became boastful. At the close of the chapter we are back again with the subtle *prāṇa* that supports all the faculties of our being, their number here limited to four. Speech represents the faculty of communicating ideas. Communication requires knowing as well as shaping what is known into a communicable form, all of which is done by senses and mind together. *Prāṇa*, thus, represents also the realm of communicating ideas and feelings.

S: How is the subtle form of *prāṇa* felt auspicious?

G: Theoretically an abstract principle, *prāṇa* becomes a direct experience in the proper functioning of all the faculties. No abstract principle is of any value unless experienced in actual life. The presence of *prāṇa* makes all life activities and all value experiences possible, and is thus considered auspicious, signified by the word *śiva*. *Prāṇa* leaving is the most inauspicious event, that which we call 'death'.

S: Being the firm basis of all our faculties, how can *prāṇa* leave them? Yet such a phenomenon is seen at the time of 'death'.

G: Really no such departing happens.

S: Do you mean that *prāṇa* leaving the body is merely imaginary?

G: The *prāṇa* functioning in an individual organism is in essence not different from the *prāṇa* functioning cosmically. This *prāṇa* is eternally functioning everywhere, and as a result new organisms emerge and old ones disappear. Even as the integration of innumerable factors into a living organism is the work of *prāṇa*, so too are its disintegration and disappearance. *Prāṇa* functions everywhere unceasingly. How can we say then that it leaves a particular being at a particular point of time? What we call death is nothing more than a part of the total transformation of the world constantly taking place. Death itself marks the emergence of something new, though indefinite, like the death of the egg is the birth of the chick. *Prāṇa*, seen thus from a holistic perspective, neither comes nor leaves. It just functions. Life goes on unceasingly. Death appears as significant only when we look at ourselves as individual entities existing by ourselves, separate from others. Even the gods who here pray to *prāṇa* are not free from such a deluded vision.

प्राणस्येदं वशे सर्वं त्रिदिवे यत् प्रतिष्ठितम् ।
मातेव पुत्रान् रक्षस्व श्रीश्च प्रज्ञां च विधेहि न इति ।। १३ ।।

prāṇasyedaṁ vaśe sarvaṁ tridive yat pratiṣṭhitam ।
māteva putrān rakṣasva śrīś ca prajñāṁ ca vidhehi na iti ।। 13 ।।

Everything in this world is under the control of *prāṇa*. All that exists in the three worlds is under the control of *prāṇa*. O Prāṇa, protect us as a mother does her children. Please grant to us prosperity and wisdom.

Seeker: This last stanza, I feel, summarises all that was taught in this chapter. Am I right?

Guru: Yes, but a further broadening of the meaning of *prāṇa* is also to be noticed. The gods no more see *prāṇa* as the all-sustaining principle, but as everything in the three worlds, this one included.

S: This chapter began with the questions, "Who is the superior among gods?" As the chapter ends we see *prāṇa* as everything, not simply as the superior god.

G: Yes. Such is the way of gradual sublimation of Upaniṣadic teachings. *Prāṇa* as *Brahman* is not merely the vital principle behind everything, but is also their existential basis. Everything in this world, and in all the worlds, is not merely animated by *prāṇa* but is a manifest appearance of *prāṇa*. Heavan, or a world hereafter, if any, also has existence derived from *prāṇa*. The non-difference of all things from *prāṇa* is implicit even in the prayer, "O Prāṇa, protect us as a mother does her children". The mother sees her children as an extension of her own being, loving and protecting them. Her love for her children is merely an extension of her love of self. *Prāṇa* also likewise loves and protects the gods and all the worlds, seeing them as various forms of his own being. This intuitive vision is the final goal of Vedānta, and we are just entering into its details.

S: Prosperity is also asked for here, over and above wisdom.

G: Yes. Wisdom and food are known to be the two extremes of the hierarchy of human values. Prosperity or *śrī* shows abundance of earthly values.

S: A mother lovingly tolerates the faults of her children. Is that relevant here?

G: Yes, to a certain extent. The gods, committed an error at the beginning; now they are begging pardon in an indirect way through this prayer. *Prāṇa* is willing to pardon them, but he wants to teach them the truth in the process.

We are now entering the third chapter. The first concentrated on the bodily emergence of beings as part of a total creative system of life. *Prāṇa* was examined in detail, in its individual and cosmic aspects in the second charpter. We go one step further and deeper in the proceeding chapter, attempting to ascertain the Reality that underlies even *prāṇa*.

Third Question

तृतीयः प्रश्नः

अथ हैनं कौसल्यश्चाश्वलायनः पप्रच्छ। भगवन् कुत एष प्राणो जायते कथमायात्यस्मिञ्छरीरे? आत्मानं वा प्रविभज्य कथं प्रातिष्ठते? केनोत्क्रमते? कथं बाह्यमभिधत्ते? कथमध्यात्ममिति ।। १ ।।

atha hainaṁ kausalyaś cāśvalāyanaḥ papraccha ।
bhagavan kuta eṣa prāṇo jāyate katham āyāty asmin śarīre? ātmānaṁ vā pravibhajya kathaṁ prātiṣṭhate? kenotkramate, kathaṁ bāhyam abhidhatte? katham adhyātmam iti ।। 1 ।।

Then Kausalya, the son of Aśvala, asked Pippalāda: Venerable Sir, whence is this *prāṇa* born? How does he come into this body? Himself divided, how does he find stability? By what means does he find stability? By what means does he depart? How does he sustain the externl? How does he sustain the self-based?

Seeker: As is clear from the five questions, we are about to examine subtler aspects of *prāṇa*. Is there anything of importance to be noticed in these questions?

Guru: Yes, there is. These questions arise from what was taught in the two previous chapters. The first chapter dealt with the physical origin of organisms, and the second examined the predominance of *prāṇa*. Of the five questions asked here, the second one is, how does *prāṇa* enter a physical body; in other words, how the factors examined in the first two chapters are interrelated. The riddle of the mind-matter relationship arises in this chapter, leading us to the non-dual Self beyond both, which is the central theme for meditation of this chapter.

S: Are these random questions, or are they interconnected?

G: Summarising what is taught in this chapter, the final verse will restate the nature of these questions as concerning the origin of *prāṇa* (*utpatti*), entry into the body (*āyāti*), stability (*sthānam*), the all-sustaining character (*vibhutvam*) and self-basedness (*adhyātmam*). The attainment of immortality is achieved by those who know one *prāṇa* in all these respects. The five questions may be considered as five distinct steps of contemplative progression rather than as five disjunct problems to be answered. Any study of this chapter has therefore to correlate the five questions and their answers meditatively.

S: It seems rather hard to accomplish.

G: Yes, it is. The wisdom of Upaniṣads is not revealed by light-hearted reading. The very word *upaniṣad* means 'secret wisdom', its secretness being the difficulty of seeing through it. We are repreatedly warned: *ātmavidyā* (Self-knowledge), the wisdom of the Upaniṣad, is rooted in *tapas* (*ātmavidyā tapomūlam*). This enquiry of ours likewise must become *tapas*.

S: *Prāṇa*, in the previous chapter (II.3), said, "Dividing myself five-fold, I sustain this arrow." Is it the same idea that is carried over as the third question here?

G: Yes, it is. The poetical genius of the *ṛṣi* uses the casual reference of a former stage to unfold a new realm of higher thought at a later stage. Similarly the reference in Stanzas 4 and 12 to *prāṇa* leaving the body, is carried over to this chapter. *Utkramaṇa* in ordinary usage means the soul leaving the body, but here the word is replaced by *vibhutva*, (the omnipresense of *prāṇa*), and so the idea of it leaving becomes meaningless. So too, the last chapter ended with the words. "All this is under the control of *prāṇa*". The 'all this' is elucidated and categorised here as the external (*bāhya*) and the self-based (*adhyātma*). Thought thus flows and develops leading to the attainment of immortality.

तस्मै स होवाचातिप्रश्नान् पृच्छसि ब्रह्मिष्ठोऽसीति तस्मात्तेऽहं ब्रवीमि ।। २ ।।

tasmai sa hovāca atipraśnān pṛcchasi, brahmiṣṭho'sīti tasmāt te'haṁ bravīmi ॥ 2 ॥

He then said to him : The question you are asking is beyond limits. Yet, seeing you yearning for nothing but *Brahman*, I shall answer you.

Seeker: The questions here arise from the thought developed in the last chapter. Why does the *guru* describe the question as beyond limits?

Guru: When do definite questions arise in our mind?

S: On feeling an urge to know clearly something that was not clear.

G: What do you mean by clear knowledge?

S: What can be explained and is also understandable in a logical manner.

G: Questions arise thus as a result of our logical thinking.

S: That is right.

G: There are certain questions which are reasonable when asked, but have no reasonable answer. Such questions are *atipraśnas* (questions beyond limits).

S: Do you mean that these questions are unanswerable?

G: No. If so Pippalāda would not have answered. Rather, we must not expect the answer to be logical, and examining the answer with a logical mind cannot unravel the intended mystical content. Pippalāda's initial hesitation in answering is a sort of warning to seekers. We have to change the tone of our thinking to follow Pippalāda.

S: What is the '*brahmiṣṭha*' Pippalāda sees Kausalya as?

G: *Brahmiṣṭha* is a person who is still yearning for the knowledge of *Brahman*, though well-versed in all the basic scriptures. He knows all the answers given in the scriptures, and is still not satisfied. The final transparency, missing in the scriptures, is to be revealed in meditation, with the scriptural utterances serving as instruments or stepping stones. Familiarity with scriptures and their expositions does not make one a *jñānin*. In calling Kausalya a *brahmiṣṭha*, Pippalāda recognises his competence to receive the rare wisdom about to be revealed here. The ancient tradition of India holds that such wisdom should be imparted only to fully competent seekers. Often the nature of their question is seen as the evidence of their competence.

S: Then what about the competence of the two seekers who were answered before?

G: As a test of their competence, all the six were asked at the beginning to stay with him a year, which they did, proving themselves competent. Now, just before entering the core of the teaching the questioner's competence is once more verified.

S: Now I feel we need to be competent enough to receive this learning.

G: Yes of course. This is something like an interlude in the course of our self-learning. We have to stop for a while, look back at ourselves, and make sure that we are indeed competent. If we are unsatisfied, we should rather wait till we acquire the necessary competence before proceeding with the learning.

आत्मन एष प्राणो जायते। यथैषा पुरुषे छायैतस्मिन्नेतदाततं
मनोकृतेनायात्यस्मिञ्छरीरे ।। ३ ।।

ātmana eṣa prāṇo jāyate । *yathaiṣā puruṣe chāyaitasminn*
etad ātataṁ manokṛtenāyāty asmin śarīre ।। 3 ।।

This *prāna* is born of the Self (*ātman*). As a person has a shadow, so too this (*prāṇa*) is pervaded by this (Self). It comes into this body through (its own) mind-activity.

Seeker: What is the *ātmā* that *prāṇa* is born of and pervaded by?

Guru: It is a word used with shades of meaning in the Upaniṣads. In the first verse of this chapter, for example, the word was used in the sense 'oneself', when it said, *ātmānam pravibhajya* (himself-divided). Here the word stands for the Absolute Reality, the all-pervading substance. The stanza itself says *ātmā* is *ātmā* because it pervades (*ātatam*) *prāṇa* which in turn controls the entire world. That which pervades *prāṇa*, in effect therefore, pervades the entire world. The birth of *prāṇa* from *ātmā* is like the birth of an ornament from gold, not like the birth of a child from a womb. As gold itself continues to exist in the form of ornaments, so too *ātmā*, the Reality, continues to exist in the *prāṇa* as well as in the entire world; no process of birth as such therefore takes place. This way of understanding the birth of everything is known as *ajātavāda* (the no-birth theory).

S: But, Pippalāda specifically says *prāṇa* is *born* of *ātmā*, which I think presupposes admitting a process of giving birth.

G: It was only to make it answer to the question, "Whence is this *prāṇa* born?" We were warned in advance that the answer was not to be understood literally, or even logically and that more-than-familiarity-with-the scriptures was required in following the line of thought.

S: Should we then take the words 'is born' as meaning 'is not born'?

G: Yes, in one sense. But that should be accompanied with the understanding of *prāṇa* as 'no-*prāṇa*' and of the world as 'no-world'. If you understood *prāṇa* as real and the world as real, then we should say *ātmā* is their source. Such a differentiation of cause and effect, of *ātmā* and the world, is meaningful only in the realm of ideas and words; it does not affect their inseparability.

S: It is easy to think of *ātmā* as the substance that pervades our being, like gold pervades ornaments. But gold is merely an inert, gross metal, whereas *ātmā* is pure Consciousness in essence. How can the two be similar?

G: Well. Have you ever seen gold as a substance in its own form, not in any given form?

S: I have seen gold in all forms of ornaments but as a substance it has no form of its own.

G: Gold as a substance is a formless entity, and invisible in its formlessness. So too is *ātmā*. Gold is the invisible substance pervading visible forms of ornaments; likewise the invisible *ātmā* pervades everything in this world. The whole range of appearances from the subtlest life principle to the grossest physical body and all that lies in between these extremes, is but an apparent form of the same *ātmā*.

Gold substance is invisible, but we know it exists, because without it the being of ornaments would be impossible. Though it remains unseen, we know gold exists. That existence is in our knowledge, as knowledge. So too *ātmā* also exists in Consciousness, as Consciousness. Melting and reshaping makes the ornament non-existent, though the gold remains. The ornament is destructible, the gold indestructible. Destruction of the visible entities in this world does not render the *ātmā* non-existent. The indestructible substance is called *sat* and its apparent destructible forms *bhāva*. *Sat* and *bhāva*, indestructible and destructible, are, to our amazement, so related that one cannot exist without the other. The indestructible gold has to exist in some destructible form; a destructible ornament can exist only with the indestructible gold for its substance; so too the indestructible *ātmā* exists in the destructible forms of the world, and the destructible world cannot become apparent in the absence of the *ātmā*.

Intuitively visualising the non-duality of *sat* and *bhāva*, is one of the secrets of *advaita* philosophy. It finds emphasis in the *Bhagavad Gītā* thus:

> The non-existent (*asat*) does not have any apparent form (*bhāva*); the existent (*sat*) does not remain without any apparent form either. That which is hidden in between the two is seen only by real philosophers. — II. 16

This inseparability of reality and appearance, in the present context, is brought out by the analogy of person and shadow. The world is represented by *prāṇa* pervaded by *ātmā*.

S: Why is man called *puruṣa*?

G: Etymologically the word means one who reposes (*śayati*) on a city (*pura*). Taking the physical body as a city, the person living in it is the *puruṣa*; in the cosmos-city, there is the cosmic *puruṣa*, sometimes called *virāṭ-puruṣa*. In ordinary usage, *puruṣa* means a male human being, the female being *strī*.

S: Which is the *puruṣa* who has a shadow, the individual or the cosmic?

G: Which was the *prāṇa* we saw in the last chapter, individual or cosmic?

S: Both together.

G: So too, *ātmā*, the *purṣua* of the analogy, is both at the same time. Just as every individual person has a shadow following, the cosmic person is followed by a shadow, the world. Is shadow visible where there is no light?

S: No.

G: Even the original figure becomes distinct only in light, and then its shadow becomes prominent. In the absence of light the original figure becomes indistinct and the shadow vanishes. So too, when the ultimate Reality is distinctly conceived, its shadow, the world, also becomes clear.

S: The word *ātatam* relating to *ātmā* and *prāṇa* seems intriguing. Which pervades which? The text simply says, "This is pervaded by this."

G: The apparent form of an ornament pervades the being of gold; and the being of gold pervades the entire form of the ornament. Likewise, *prāṇa*, the apparent form, pervades *ātmā*; the *ātmā*-substance pervades *prāṇa*. 'That which is *ātatam* (pervasive) is *ātmā*' is a new definition this Upaniṣad gives of *ātmā*. This pervasiveness is a sign of its own creativity, a creativity that decides for itself how it should and should not unfold, the function we call mind (*manas*).

S: Usually we think of mind as that which decides what to do and what not to do. What we now see is that the function of *ātmā*, deciding how to unfold its own creativity, is called mind. These two views do not agree.

G: The former is the traditional view we are taught from childhood, leading to our preconception of a mind that thinks, imagines and performs other psychological functions, consciously or unconsciously, which is sometimes vaguely conceived as 'psyche'. Our *r̥ṣis*, not subjected to such conditioning, go deeper into what causes the emergence of *manas* (psyche). The primeval cause, the Self (*ātmā*), according to them, originally had in it the desire to see for itself its own potential actualised, and the outcome of this desire is called *manas*. The outcome of the creativity of *ātmā*, *manas* is creative by itself. *Manas* is thus a creative expression of *ātmā*, and *prāṇa* which here represents everything, is a creative expression of *manas* — all of this is implicit in the unique usage *manokr̥ta* (mind-activity).

Prāṇa attains a body through the activity of this mind, not at random. *Manas* emerged from the primeval desire in *ātmā*, and creative as it is, assumed grossness to become body, comparable to gold assuming the form of an ornament. *Prāṇa*, *manas*, *śarīra* (body) are all various stages in which the one and only *ātmā* finds self-expression — "It comes into this body through its own mind-activity."

S: Do you mean that this physical body is merely a mental image?

G: Yes, I do. That gold, the substance in all ornaments, exists only in and as consciousness we have already seen. The apparent visible forms also do not exist apart from consciousness or *manas*.

S: Could you please make it clearer?

G: Here, for instance, is a rose. Do you recognise it as a rose?

S: Yes, of course, I do.

G: Suppose you have never seen a rose before. Would you then recognise this as a rose?

S: No.

G: Why?

S: Because the idea of rose was not in my mind.

G: That means, to recognise something the idea must already be in the mind.

S: That is true.

G: Recognising is thus the act of re-cognising something already cognised.

S: Yes.

G: Then do you, on recognising something, see something perceived by your eyes, or do you see the object by projecting on to it a memory?

S: It is the latter.

G: What is perceived then, in the act of recognising, is something in our mind, rather than something existing out there.

S: Still some object exists out there and we perceive it.

G: Yes, that is true. Here is the object we call 'rose'. You can see its petalled form, smell its fragrance, touch its softness and sense many such qualities. All these sensations are of the qualities of the rose. The shape, fragrance, softness, are all qualities, and none by itself is the rose. All your sense-contact is with these qualities, but what you mentally perceive is the rose, the qualified. Where is the qualified, the rose, then? Is it out there or in your mind?

S: I should say it is in my mind.

G: Those aspects of the rose that senses are in contact with are all qualities which exist because the qualified exists. If the qualified is in the mind, then where do the qualities exist?

S: They are also in the mind. What is it I see before me then?

G: It is merely a configuration of the mind — *manokṛta*.

S: How is that possible?

G: Your own mind has in it the potential to materialise as this rose, its numerous qualities, objects like this rose and their qualities, in short the whole world and all its qualities. This hidden potential of consciousness to unfold itself as everything is what is called *māyā*. Narayana Guru calls this aspect of Pure Consciousness, the one Mind whose imaginations get materialized as all things — *adhyātmasthūla-saṁkalpanā*.

यथा सम्राडेवाधिकृतान् विनियुङ्क्ते। एतान् ग्रामानेतान् ग्रामानधि-
तिष्ठस्वेत्येवमेवैष प्राण इतरान् प्राणान् पृथक्पृथगेव सन्निधत्ते ॥ ४ ॥

yathā samrāḍ evādhikṛtān viniyuṅkte । *etān grāmān etān grāmān adhitiṣṭhasvety evam evaiṣa prāṇa itarān prāṇān pṛthak pṛthag eva sannidhatte* ॥ 4 ॥

As an emperor commands his officials saying, "Superintendent such and such districts", even so this *prāṇa* directs other *prāṇas* in their respective functions.

Seeker: Does Pippalāda answer all the five questions in their order?

Guru: Yes, Kausalya asked five questions, and at the very outset Pippalāda pointed out the uniqueness of the questions, which is to be seen in the answers also. The previous stanza answered the first two questions. Seemingly distinct from one another, these answers are to be intuitively and meditatively perceived as revealing a holistic vision. This stanza answers the third question.

S: *Prāṇa* emanated from *ātmā*. Why can't then we say that *ātmā* directs the different *prāṇa*s to their duties?

G: That would at first glance seem to be the better way of putting it. As *ātmā* is the causal reality even of *prāṇa*, the vitality of life, *ātmā* has to be above even *prāṇa* and therefore also actionless. Inhering the potential to unfold as everything, *ātmā* is actionless. When this potential actualises it is no more *ātmā*, but is *prāṇa*. All activities are therefore conceived as taking place in *prāṇa*, which is the shadow to *ātmā*, the attributeless (*nirviśeṣa*) and unconditioned (*nirupādhika*) Reality. All functions belong to the shadow. This principle finds expression in Indian mythological legend (*purāṇa*) in Viṣṇu, from whose navel was born Brahmā, who in turn did the actual creation of the world.

S: We are now thinking of *ātmā*, the cause even of *prāṇa*. Why should we then go back and think of *prāṇa* again?

G: The Ultimate Reality is to be intuitively visualised in and through all its manifest forms (*bhāvas*). *Prāṇa* is the subtlest manifest form of *ātmā*. It is the subtlest functions of *prāṇa* that we are seeing through now. In order that *ātmā* becomes transparent we have to view it through the subtle functioning of *prāṇa* — another unreasonable aspect of the method of approach in this chapter.

Even as *ātmā* remains invisible, veiled by its own manifest forms, so too, the secret teaching of an Upaniṣad is veiled by its own words. A contemplative seeker has to see through these words and get at the Reality underneath, in the two stages of *manana* and *nididhyāsana*. No more explicit reference to *ātmā* is going to be seen in this Upaniṣad. While *ātmā* being all that is intended, reference to it as the source of *prāṇa* is all that is needed to help a seeker in his *manana* and *nididhyāsana*. As further aid, the rest of the chapter goes into the details of the functions of *prāṇa*. Even the name of this Upaniṣad is *Praśna Upaniṣad*. *Praśna* means question, problem, point of issue, even conundrum. The core of the conundrum-like teaching concealed by these words has to be discovered. Pippalāda also warned in advance that Kausalya's question went beyond limits. I think this riddle could be simplified if represented graphically.

S: How?

G: The usage of graphs is familiar to us in mathematics and statistics. Graph has a vertical axis as well as a horizontal axis. The invisible, actionless *ātmā* could be represented by the vertical axis and all its variously manifest forms such as *prāṇa* and its diversified functions by the horizontal axis. The secret teaching of non-duality could then be considered represented by the neutral point where the two axes meet.

S: This stanza being concerned with the diversification of *prāṇa*'s functions, why can't we think of *prāṇa* as symbolised by the vertical axis and its diversified functions by the horizontal axis?

G: That would be correct if the matter of our concern here was *prāṇa* and its functions. These are two different frames of reference of thought (*prakaraṇas*). Clear scientific thinking, to be saved from the pitfall of mixing up of ideas, requires an understanding of the frame of reference to which the particular topic belongs, in turn necessitating prior knowledge of the overall scheme of the concerned work. The present Upaniṣad, for example, in its first chapter, deals with the birth of an individual as part of a total scheme of life. The next chapter follows with *prāṇa* as the all-sustaining vitality in any organism. The present chapter goes one step deeper to *ātmā* as the source even of *prāṇa*. The discussion in this chapter in hinged on how *ātmā* unfolds itself in the form of the various functions of *prāṇa*. The next chapter will concentrate on the various functions of consciousness, the essential content of *ātmā*. Details of certain practical disciplines aimed at attaining the reality of *ātmā* is the theme of the fifth chapter. The final chapter visualises *ātmā* again as *puruṣa*, but this time as having sixteen *kalā*s. Thought, till the preceding stanza, was of an ascending order, starting with the physical emergences of beings and reaching the sublimity of *ātmā*. We will see a descending order in the development of thought from the present stanza onwards, beginning with seeing *ātmā* in the subtle functions of *prāṇa* and finally seeing the same *ātmā* in all the constituent elements of beings. Details of the development of thought are different in different scriptural texts like Upaniṣads. What the core of the teaching is, how the *ṛṣi* develops it, how it begins, where it attains its zenith, how it concludes — should all be clear in the mind of a serious student of any scripture.

Let us now go back to the text itself.

S: *Prāṇa*, the all-sustaining vitality, is aptly compared to an emperor.

G: But we should not miss the principle of *ātmā* behind it, the principle that confers emperorhood on *prāṇa*. An emperor's concern is ensuring the well-being of his subjects. *Prāṇa* also does the same; it sustains all the vital functions in every organism. It also keeps the integrity and unity of the cosmic system, while maintaining the eternal flux of nature. These functions are of a more physical and transactional nature like the functions of an emperor. But there is a principle that unites emperor and subject, and though not transactional, in its absense no emperor can be an emperor, and no subject a subject. So too, no *prāṇa* is *prāṇa* in its absense. No thing is what it is, in the absense of *ātmā*.

S: An emperor rules his empire not directly, but through his deputies who are like his limbs. *Prāṇa* also likewise deputes other *prāṇa*s to be his functionaries. Are these other *prāṇas* to be viewed as the main *prāṇa*'s limbs?

G: Yes. The other *prāṇa*s, though referred to as 'other' are not really 'other'; simply diversified functions of the one *prāṇa*, differently named. All the officials do their business with full awareness of the intention of the emperor, the other *prāṇa*s also function with full awareness of the structural unity of the whole organism. Billions of cells, each with its own structural integrity and functional peculiarity, ensure the structural coherence of a body. The memory of the total structure of the body is contained in each cell. To put the same in the terminology of the Upaniṣad, the integrity of the vital functions of the chief *prāṇa* is inherent in each of the other *prāṇa*s. This overall system that unites the one chief *prāṇa* and all the other *prāṇa*s into one total life unit of consciousness is *ātmā*, where the *cit* aspect becomes dominant over the *sat* aspect.

पायूपस्थेऽपानं चक्षुःश्रोत्रे मुखनासिकाभ्यां प्राणः स्वयं प्रातिष्ठते मध्ये तु
समानः। एषह्येतद्धुतमन्नं समं नयति तस्मादेताः सप्तार्चिषो भवन्ति ॥ ५ ॥

pāyūpasthe'pānaṁ cakṣuḥ śrotre mukha-nāsikābhyāṁ prāṇaḥ svayaṁ prātiṣṭhate madhye tu samānaḥ । *eṣa hy etadd hutam annaṁ samaṁ nayati tasmād etāḥ saptārciṣo bhavanti* ॥ 5 ॥

To the excretory organ and genitals (is directed) *apāna* (the downward vital function). *Prāṇa* himself functions in the eyes and ears, in the mouth and nose. *Samāna* (equalising vital function) that distributes indeed equitably whatever is offered as food, is directed to the middle region; from it arises the seven flames.

Seeker: How are the functions of *prāṇa* divided?

Guru: The functions of *prāṇa* are conceived variously in different texts. The vital functions of an organism are many. Different perspectives lead to different classifications, but the functions are always five in number. The details of the five in one text therefore need not necessarily agree with those of another.

S: Why is *apāna* conceived as functioning in the exceretory organ and genitals?

G: The very word *apāna* has a negative connotation, implying negative activity. The negative activity of eliminating something happens through these two organs and is hence conceived as the seat of *apāna*. *Apāna* functioning ensures the homeostasis of an organism by eliminating unwanted or excess material and mental factors.

S: Is there a mental excretion also?

G: Yes, there is. A mind, tense with day long monotonies, gets a feeling of release, after a sort of mental excretion, on having some fun or entertainment. People sometimes let go of all restraints at fairs and festivals enjoying the occasion, and get release from sediments of the boring formalities of customary life. This is the way *apāna* works mentally.

S: *Prāṇa*, as I understood, is the opposite of *apāna*. How is it conceived as functioning in the eyes and ears?

G: Grasping something is the opposite of eliminating something. All the senses, represented here by the eyes and ears, grasp the objects external and transform them into inner experiences. This is made possible, as imagined here, by *prāṇa*.

S: The main function of *prāṇa* being respiration, it is understandable how the nose and mouth became its abodes. Some textbooks say that the function of *prāṇa* is breathing in and of *apāna* breathing out. Why is there this inconsistency among textbooks?

G: Textbooks of the various systems of spiritual practice and philosophy, as I told you, describe the functions of *prāṇa* and *apāna* in accordance with their own system. *Haṭha Yoga*, for example, the Yoga system that gives primacy to the practice called *prāṇāyāma* (breathe control), considers breathing in as the function of *prāṇa* and breathing out as that of *apāna*. Those systems which are more concerned with body metabolism think the respiratory function is owing to *prāṇa* and the downward discharge of air through the anus as the function of *apāna*. There are other variations too, in accordance with the central values of each system. Revealing the non-dual *ātmā* is the central theme of the Upaniṣads, and *prāṇa* is seen here as the primeval creative self-expression of *ātmā*. The *prāṇa*, in turn, in its five-fold functions, sustains the entire organism. It does not mean that *prāṇa*'s functions are only five; they are simply grouped into five. What is important here is visualising the whole of life as a creative process sustained by *prāṇa* through its diversified functions. So the number of *prāṇa*s and their respective functions are less significant.

At the centre of such a system is the *samāna*, the vitality that distributes energy equitably to all parts of the body. Reminiscent of the Vedic offerings carried to the gods by fire, food is treated here as an offering whose essence is carried by *samāna* to the respective parts. On consuming food the latent happiness (*ānanda*) in us becomes actualised and experienced, like latent energy becoming explicit on fuel being consumed by fire.

S: But the final aim of sacrificial offering is getting the blessings of the gods and not the releasing of energy.

G: You are right. But gods and their blessings are merely sysmbols. Gods symbolise expressed forms of knowledge as we have already seen in detail. *Devas* (gods) mean, those with the essence of brightness; fire is bright; knowledge is an experience of brightness. Blessings of the gods attained through *yajñas* therefore signify the contentment attained through wisdom. The arising of seven flames (*saptārcis*) stands for the seven ways in which knowledge finds expression. Narayana Guru in his *Homa Mantram* sees the five senses, mind and intellect as the seven tongues (*sapta jihvāḥ*) of the fire of consciousness. Neither consciousness nor *prāṇa* can function without the energy gained from food.

S: The energy derived from food being what sustains our *prāṇa* as well as consciousness, could we think that the quality of food we eat changes our character?

G: Certainly.

हृदि ह्येष आत्मा। अत्रैतदेकशतं नाडीनां तासां शतं शतमेकैकस्यां द्वासप्ततिर्द्वासप्ततिः प्रतिशाखानाडीसहस्राणि भवन्त्यासु व्यानश्चरति ।। ६ ।।

hṛdi hy eṣa ātmā । atraitad ekaśataṁ nāḍīnāṁ, tāsāṁ śataṁ śatam ekaikasyāṁ dvāsaptatir dvāsaptatiḥ pratiśākhā-nāḍī-sahasrāṇi bhavanty āsu vyānaś carati ।। 6 ।।

In the heart is this (*samāna*'s) self. From here are issued one hundred and one arteries. Of each one of them are issued a hundred smaller arteries. Of each of these branches are issued seventytwo thousand sub-branches. Within all these move *vyāna* (the diffused breath).

Seeker: This stanza details *vyāna* and its functions. Why is then the word *eṣaḥ* (this) at the beginning taken as referring to *samāna* of the previous stanza.

Guru: A rule of Sanskrit diction is that the word *eṣaḥ* at the beginning of a sentence or verse refers to what was described just before. References to *vyāna* comes only at the end of this stanza, after first detailing its functions. It would therefore be apt to take the word *eṣaḥ* as denoting *samāna*. Such an interpretation will also reveal how the function of *samāna* and *vyāna* are sequential : distribution of vitality assimilated from food is followed by blood circulation and functions of the nervous system, the function of *vyāna*.

S: What is meant by *hṛt* rendered as heart here? Is it the blood-pumping organ? Or is it the source of feelings, imagined by literature?

G: We are not sure whether the circulatory and nervous systems were biologically differentiated when the Upaniṣads were written. The vision of the *ṛṣis* was a holistic one in which body and mind are inseparable. But they speak of distribution of vitality, circulation of blood and sensory functions as parallels. That these are various functions of one *prāṇa* is the vision conceived here. The *hṛt* (heart) therefore is the centre of the circulatory and nervous systems, the source of emotions and feelings, all put together—the core of individual being undivided as mind and matter.

S: How can this heart be the self of *samāna*?

G: *Ātmā* (self), we know, is a word used in the Upaniṣad with different connotations. Heart, as the seat of *samāna*'s focal point of activities, is thought of as its *ātmā*; at the same time it is the focal point of activities (*ātmā*) of *vyāna* also. Ultimately *samāna* and *vyāna* are nothing more than two functional modes of one *prāṇa* born of *ātmā*; therefore not different from *ātmā*.

S: The *prāṇa-apāna* pair also, in that sense, is not different from *ātmā*.

G: Though two functional modes of one *prāṇa*, perhaps because they are not spread out over the system, their non-difference from *ātmā*, does not find emphasis here, but it is not to be ruled out.

S: One hundred and one arteries issuing from this *ātmā*, the heart, each branching into a hundred, which further branch out into 7200, all these look rather like a poetical image than actual physiological details.

G: The *ṛṣi* presents here a simple intuitive vision of the functions of an organism with a place for known physiological details. The number of arteries and nerves is insignificant; what is important is the interrelatedness of the digestive, circulatory and nervous systems in a cohesive whole. Modern knowledge of the human body reveals that millions and millions of cells — represented here by the figure one hundred and one multiplied by one hundred and again by 7200 — are nourished by the circulatory system and are interlinked by a nervous system. While we cannot be sure of the extent of the ṛṣi's knowledge of cells, we are here given sure evidence of the ṛiṣi's knowledge of the organism as a whole in which countless parts are indivisibly integrated and vitalised, the vitalisation being the function of *vyāna*.

अथैकयोर्ध्व उदानः पुण्येन पुण्यं लोकं नयति।
पापेन पापमुभाभ्यामेव मनुष्यलोकम् ॥ ७ ॥

athaikayordhva udānaḥ puṇyena puṇyaṁ lokaṁ nayati ।
pāpena pāpam ubhābhyām eva manuṣyalokam ॥ 7 ॥

Now, *udāna* (the upward breath) is that which moves upwards alone. Following meritorious deeds it leads to the world of merits; following sinful deeds it leads to the world of sins. Following both kinds of deeds it leads to the human world.

Seeker: From where does *udāna*, move upwards and whereto?

Guru: *Udāna* is conceived of by Indians as the *prāṇa* that leaves the body at death, making its way through the summit of the head.

S: But no mention of death is made here?

G: That is what makes the stanza a bit of a puzzle, and the words "it leads to the world of merits" makes it more so. Usually the stanza is, interpreted thus: *udāna* leads the soul of the dead to the world of pleasures, called *svarga* (heaven), or to the world of pains called *naraka* (hell) in accordance with the merits or sins acquired during life here in the present world.

S: No waiting until death is needed, I think, to attain heaven or hell. Such consequences are seen and felt even in this present life. We come across many men and women who make a heaven or hell of their life simply owing to their deeds, physical, verbal or mental.

G: You are right. What such men and women have is not any upward or downward going after death; rather is their own uplift or downfall in the world of values here on earth. Understanding the movement of *udāna* in that sense seems more appropriate.

S: What are then the meritorious deeds?

G: The deeds done as a spontaneous self-unfoldment of nature, or the activities taking place unavoidably in life as part of the onward flow of nature, could be considered meritorious in the absolutist sense. This concept of merit of the wisdom context may not agree with ritualistic concepts of religious merit. One may get involved in activities motivated by one's own personal interest completely forgetting that one is part of nature and overlooking the existence of others who are likewise part of nature. Such activities, in the eye of wisdom, are seen as being sinful, and make hell of one's life, even though it may at times look glorious. It is often very late before one becomes aware of the trap one was caught in. The incorrigible wrongs committed, the guilty conscience, all weigh down on life. One who is aware of the one Reality, will do and can do only those deeds which ensure one's own and all others' happiness. Such deeds are ethically sound and are meritorius. Those deeds which, while ensuring one's own happiness cause sufferings to others, in this sense, are sinful.

S: Do you mean that what we call heaven and hell are mere value worlds, not actually existing?

G: They do exist actually as value worlds and they will have place in human life as long as it is ruled by values. That is the reason why these worlds had found place in all religions. Even the religious concept of these worlds is merely of value significance.

S: Could you please explain?

G: What kind of life is expected in heaven?

S: A happy life only.

G: We conceive of heavenly happiness with worldly happiness as the criterion. Right?

S: Yes, of course.

G: Heaven, then, is imagined as the abode of all that is best in this world.

S: It should be so.

G: So too, hell is the world full of all the worst imaginable things of this world. The pleasures and pains of these two worlds have never been experienced by anyone other than in the imagination while living in this world (*manuṣya loka*).

S: That is true.

G: Heaven and hell thus exist as ideas of total happiness and total suffering, in the human mind while living in this human world. *Udāna* could in that sense be thought of as either the human inner longing for higher values, or the urge that pulls one down to the infatuations of lower values. It can even be seen as the urge that keeps one in the realm where both these urges are normal — the human world.

S: Do you mean that the movement of *udāna* is both upwards and downwards, though only the upward movement is referred to?

G: Yes, the concept of upward movement has implicit in it the concept of the downward movement. Only those who know what cold is, will be able to appreciate warmth. So too, only those who can think of an underworld of lower values can understand and appreciate the upper world of higher values. In the present case, though only the upward movement is mentioned first, it is followed by the reference to *udāna* leading to the sinful world, no doubt, a downward movement.

S: Why should the world of merits be up above and the world of sins down below?

G: It is a concept held by all religions, not supported by any reason. Yet the human mind cannot think otherwise.

S: Could you please clarify it?

G: If a person much respected by all, comes to a gathering, what kind of seat will he be offered?

S: The most respectable and highest seat.

G: Why can't the respectable seat be placed at the lowest spot?

S: It will be considered awkward; such a thing is unimaginable.

G: The respect or value we give to something or somebody and the height at which they are placed are related, though we don't know why. In the human mind everything conceived as of high value is always placed at a high position. Heaven, where reside the highest worldly values, is seen higher than all other worlds. So too, the world of the lowest values is placed beneath all other worlds. Yet the loftiness or baseness of these worlds is meaningful only in the human world in between, which is a combination of the two.

S: Why is the movement of *udāna* a lone one?

G: The function of all the other *prāṇas* being biological, that of *udāna*, which is more of value significance, is not related to them.

अदित्यो ह वै बाह्यः प्राण उदयत्येष ह्येनं चाक्षुषं प्राणमनुगृह्णानः।
पृथिव्यां या देवता सैषा पुरुषस्यापानमवष्टभ्यान्तरा यदाकाशः स समानो
वायुर्व्यानः ॥ ८ ॥

तेजो ह वाव उदानस्तस्मादुपशान्ततेजाः पुनर्भवमिन्द्रियैर्मनसि
संपद्यमानैः ॥ ९ ॥

ādityo ha vai bāhyaḥ prāṇa udayaty, eṣa hy enaṁ cākṣuṣaṁ prāṇam anugr̥hṇānaḥ । *pr̥thivyāṁ yā devatā saiṣā puruṣasyāpānam avaṣṭabhyāntarā yad ākāśaḥ sa samāno, vāyur vyānaḥ* ॥ 8 ॥

tejo ha vāva udānas, tasmād upaśāntatejāḥ punarbhavam indriyair manasi sampadyamānaiḥ ॥ 9 ॥

The sun, verily, as the externally manifest *prāṇa*, rises gracing the *prāṇa* of eyes. The divinity in the earth siezes *apāna* in man. What is in between (the sun and the earth) is *samāna* and air is *vyāna*.

Fire verily is *udāna*. Because of it, one, whose lustre has died out, with senses sunk in mind, re-emerges.

Seeker: The functions of *prāṇa*, *apāna*, *samāna*, *vyāna*, and *udāna* having already been covered in the stanzas just examined, why should it be repeated here?

Guru: The functions of the five *prāṇas* described so far are related to every individual's being. Now we look at the same *prāṇas* as operating universally in the cosmic system.

S: Why are these two aspects of function separately examined?

G: *Prāṇa*, conceived singly in Chapter II, was also seen as functioning both in the universal and particular aspects of existence. Here, in this chapter, dealing with the details of the same *prāṇa*, also, the dual functional faces have to be clarified. The real intention of this double-faced description is more to enable us to see for ourselves the unitive function of the *prāṇa*'s five divisions, than to give us a detailed knowledge of them.

S: It is not clear.

G: We saw under Stanza II. 6 how appearance and reality are inseparable in non-dual existence. *Prāṇa* and its functions are also to be intuitively visualised in the same way. Universal function and particular function, though seemingly different, are like the two faces of a coin, neither of which is the reality; the reality is the coin. So too, neither cosmic brightness of the sun nor the individual brightness of eyes is the real function of *prāṇa*. The one function which has these for its two opposing faces is the Real. The sun's brightness helps us see things in this world distinctly. A shining sun in the absence of the eye is valueless. A shining eye in the absence of light is equally valueless. *Prāṇa*, here one of the five aspects of the chief *prāṇa*, functions keeping the sun shining in the cosmos and the eye in human body, actualising the event of perception. The eye here stands for all the senses mentioned in Stanza 5.

S: How is *apāna* related to the earth?

G: The downward vital force *apāna* functions in the excretory and genital organs. We see a similar downward force in the earth's gravitational pull, in water seeping down into the earth, and in physical bodies going back to it after death — these are all universal functions of *apāna*.

Samāna was seen located in the middle region of the body, so too its universal aspect is seen in the middle region of the world, space (*ākāśa*).

The function of *samāna* is distributing vitality equitably throughout the body. Its universal aspect is the distribution going on in the world through air. *Udāna* helps upward movement to the world of higher values. The universal phenomenon that always moves upwards is fire, and therefore fire is the universal aspect of *udāna*.

S: The word used here for fire is *tejas* which also means brightness. Is this usage significant in that sense?

G: Yes. Life is recognised as a sort of brightness; its burning out is death. But the dying out of fire at one instance does not mean the extinction of fire as a universal phenomenon. So too, the dying out of the fire of life in one person does not mean the extinction of life. It re-emerges in some other new form. The text therefore says, "One whose lustre has died out, with senses sunk in mind, re-emerges."

S: Does it imply what is understood as re-incarnation?

G: Yes, but in the philosophical or rather ontological sense as conceived by the Upaniṣads. Even when something disappears, its inner content cannot simply vanish. It has to continue to exist in some other form. This second form in which it re-appears is a re-emergence (*punar bhavam*) of the former. The gold in an ornament, when reshaped by a goldsmith, re-emerges in a new form.

S: Here we are not concerned with the disappearence and re-emergence of physical bodies like ornaments, but with the function of *udāna* as the lustre of life.

G: *Prāṇa* of which *udāna* is only a functional aspect, is merely an animating principle in an individual being; it is the vital principle that keeps life eternally flowing, finding expression in its endless facets, simplified here as five. The dying out of the lustre of life in our being does not mean the cessation of life. It merges in the cosmic brilliance to find other individual expressions. Universally *prāṇa* does not cease to function, only its individual facets appear and disappear.

S: Why can't we take this merger and re-emergence as taking place in *ātmā* itself?

G: Though correct in a general sense, such a way of looking at it does not fit in with the way of presentation adopted in this Upaniṣad. *Ātmā*, the source even of *prāṇa*, when active, is no more *ātmā*, but is *prāṇa*: the only difference between the two according to the method of approach of this Upaniṣad. Emergence, transformations and merger of individual forms take place in the domain of activities, in *prāṇa*; *ātmā* remaining attributeless, actionless unconditioned and unmanifested. For this reason no description of *ātmā* is given in this Upaniṣad; what is defined or described is only whatever manifests from *ātmā*, *prāṇa* being the most subtle and vital of these manifestations.

S: It is said, "One, whose lustre has died out with senses sunk in mind, re-emerges." What does it mean? Whose mind is it?

G: A general belief prevailing among Indians is that the senses and incipient memories (*vāsanās*) of the one who dies merge in his own mind, forming a subtle body (*sūkṣma śarīra*), and after drifting in the atmosphere and many worlds, it is reborn in a new gross body. But the present stanza does not subscribe to such an idea. *Prāṇa* is the source of all transformations; the senses are only minute elements of such transformations. Mind, the controller of all senses, is another mode in which *prāṇa* functions. We have just noticed how the universal, eternal functions of *prāṇa* are inseparable from individual aspects. The disappearance of individual brightness does not mean the extinction of universal brightness. Individual lustre merges into its own universal, eternal aspect which is always in the act of emanating new facets of brightness. The emergence of a new form of brightness is possible only at the disappearance of a former one, as the appearance of the chick is possible only with the disappearance of the egg.

Everything considered here has universal and individual facets, so too the mind has two facets. The real mind is non-dual and finds expression as these two facets.

S: Then what about the *karmas* and *vāsanās* of individuals believed to be continuing in individuals born later?

G: It is not merly a belief; it is a scientific fact. You go to a beach and watch how the waves break on the shore and recede. The force of one breaker approaching the shore and receding, you will notice, determines the force of the one that follows — the *karma* of one breaker decides the *karma* of those that follow. This is also true of the incessant wave formation in the beginningless and endless ocean of becoming — the world. All that we happen to do, think or say, leaves indelible impressions in our being, as well as in the being of others around us, encoded in our genes. These genes in turn carry them on to the next generation. Many such peculiarities gathered in the genes might be dropped off in the process of transmission from generation to generation, and new ones picked up.

S: But this is not the rebirth understood by believers. The *prāṇa* in each person, they think, along with the *karmas* and incipient memories (*vāsanās*), leaves the body of the dead and enters a new womb to be reborn.

G: Only those who do not care to understand the essential teachings of scriptures maintain such a belief. No search for truth should be on the basis of popular beliefs, but should be based on scriptural teachings and one's own contemplation.

यच्चित्तस्तेनैष प्राणमायाति, प्राणस्तेजसा युक्तः। सहात्मना यथासंकल्पितं लोकं नयति ॥ १० ॥

yac cittas tenaiṣa prāṇam āyāti, prāṇas tejasā yuktaḥ ।
sahātmanā yathā saṁkalpitaṁ lokaṁ nayati ॥ 10 ॥

As one's thinking is so he attains *prāṇa*. *Prāṇa* functions undifferentiated from lustre. Along with *ātmā*, it leads the world as mind conceives.

Seeker: *Citta*, a new concept, appears here. Where is it from?

Guru: We have been examining the functions of *prāṇa* of which lustre as the sign of life was the last one. *Prāṇa* is *ātmā* in the functional state. As *ātmā* is Consciousness, the function of *prāṇa* is the function of Consciousness also. *Citta* is that function of consciousness which recalls its own prior activities — (i.e., memory) — and hopes and plans for better future activities, all guided by a value notion. After defining the function of *prāṇa* as the sign of life, we take one step further and see how *prāṇa*, as thinking, leads life processes through imagination and planning.

S: Is it the individual mind or cosmic mind that thinks and plans?

G: Just as the other functions of *prāṇa* were seen neutrally, so the mind too is neutral but functions both as individual and cosmic.

S: It is said, "As one's thinking is so he attains *prāṇa*." What does it mean?

G: The second question asked by Kausalya at the beginning is, "How does *prāṇa* come into this body?" The answer was that *prāṇa* transformed itself as body, meaning one does not enter the other. What we conceive as body and *prāṇa* have never existed separate. We merely conceive of the two as distinct. It is then it becomes appropriate to say that *prāṇa* enters the body or *vice-versa*. For this reason it was asked, "How does *prāṇa* come into this body?" Here is an answer in reverse order. "As one's thinking is, one attains *prāṇa*." Instead of *prāṇa* entering body it says that an individual being attains *prāṇa* as its thinking is. This reversal suggests the meaninglessness of the concept of one entering or attaining the other.

Prāṇa, on the one side is inseparable from *ātmā*, its causal Reality, and on the other from its various functions. Imagining, thinking and valuing, mind, one of the functional modes of *prāṇa*, plays a crucial role in deciding the nature of life, individual and cosmic. The nature of the the world depends upon how we think of it, just as the nature of one's own life depends upon how one thinks of it.

य एवं विद्वान् प्राणं वेद। न हास्य प्रजा हीयतेऽमृतो भवति तदेष श्लोकः ।। ११ ।।

उत्पत्तिमायतिं स्थानं विभुत्वं चैव पञ्चधा ।
अध्यात्मं चैव प्राणस्य विज्ञायामृतमश्नुते विज्ञायामृतमश्नुत इति ।। १२ ।।

ya evaṁ vidvān prāṇaṁ veda । *na hāsya prajā hīyate 'mṛto bhavati tad eṣa ślokaḥ* ।। 11 ।।

utpattim āyatiṁ sthānaṁ vibhutvaṁ caiva pañcadhā ।
adhyātmaṁ caiva prāṇasya vijñāyāmṛtam aśnute vijñāyāmṛtam aśnuta iti ।। 12 ।।

The wise one, knowing *prāṇa* thus, his progeny never terminates. He becomes immortal. As to this there is this verse:

Knowing *prāṇa*'s birth, entrance, abode, five-fold all-

> pervasiveness and relation to the Self in detail, one becomes immortal! On knowing in detail one becomes immortal!

Seeker: These two stanzas together sound like another *phalaśruti*. Never terminating progeny is the benefit it promises to the wise one. How is it possible?

Guru: All the six seekers who approached Pippalāda had an ultimate goal. What was it?

S: It was to know the immortal Reality and to realise their own immortality.

G: This quest for immortality is there in everyone, don't you think?

S: Yes, all of us wish to be immortal, though it be impossible.

G: How is it attainable, as the Upaniṣads teach?

S: Knowing the Reality underlying all things and oneself as immortal, we also become immortal.

G: Those who are ignorant of this Reality can also actualise their immortality, but in a different way, through biologically begetting offspring.

S: Though that may be considered a kind of immortality, it is not that which is intended by the Upaniṣads.

G: But the present Upaniṣad admits it here. Begetting children is the earthly way of immortalising oneself. Though the Upaniṣads teach the transcendental way, the earthly is not to be fully ruled out from transcendental immortality.

S: Why?

G: You know, life on earth continues without ceasing, in spite of the mortality of its living beings.

S: Yes, that is true.

G: Would that be possible without the begetting of offspring?

S: No.

G: Procreation also is to be seen as an inevitable part of the life system, the unfoldment of the Self-Reality.

S: Yes, of course.

G: How can it be possible then to exclude from Reality, the progeny engendered by us?

S: We cannot.

G: The Upaniṣads, for this reason, do not exclude the biological necessity of procreation from the all-inclusive scope of Reality. That a basic distinction exists between the understandings of the ignorant and the wise, with respect to this biological immortality is to be noticed. The ignorant, even when actualising immortality, are not aware of their deathlessness, while the wise see the blossoming of the one immortal Reality in both the attainment of wisdom and in the earthly act of procreation.

S: Stanza 12, quoting another *ṛṣi*, speaks of brith, entrance, abode, five-fold all-pervasiveness, and relation to the Self. How are these relevant here?

G: These are exactly the five points Kausalya wanted at the beginning to be clarified. Such a quotation helps us also to review the points dealt with in this chapter.

Recapitulating and reviewing these five points: *prāṇa*, as stated in Stanza 3, was born of *ātmā*. The entry of *prāṇa* into the body is through the activity of mind, a function of the very same *prāṇa*. *Prāṇa* then was shown as directing itself through subsidiary functions — of *prāṇa*, *apāna*, *samāna*, *vyāna*, and *udāna*.

Finally in Stanza 10 *prāṇa* was seen as the vital link between *ātmā* and the five subsidiary *prāṇa*s.

S: How can this be detailed knowledge?

G: *Jñāna* (wisdom) and *vijñāna* (applied wisdom) are different. To be aware that one Reality underlies all appearances is wisdom (*jñāna*). Perceiving each and every entity we encounter in this world as a particular form in which one Reality appears, is *vijñāna* (applied wisdom), rendered here as 'knowing in detail'. How *prāṇa* originated from *ātmā* and how all the five functionaries of *prāṇa* pertain to a whole, clarified in the present chapter, are themselves details of this applied wisdom.

S: *Amṛta* and *amṛtatva* are two words that appear in the Upaniṣads whenever the final goal of Vedānta is referred to. What do they actually mean?

G: *Mṛtyu* means death; *mṛta* means the dead; its opposite is *amṛta*. *Amṛtatva* is the state of having no death. The individual mortal being, becoming aware, "I am one with the immortal Self", just as each wave is aware "I am one with the ocean", is the essence of the attainment of *amṛtatva*.

S: The sentence, "Knowing in detail one becomes immortal" is repeated. Why is it so?

G: Repeating the last sentence to indicate the end of the chapter, or of the whole work, as the case may be, by reiterating the core of the teaching or the ultimate value of the teaching, is customary in most of the Upaniṣads.

Fourth Question

चतुर्थः प्रश्नः

अथ हैनं सौर्यायणी गार्ग्यः पप्रच्छ। भगवन्नेतस्मिन् पुरुषे कानि स्वपन्ति? कान्यस्मिञ्जाग्रति? कतर एष देवः स्वप्नान् पश्यति? कस्यैतत्सुखं भवति? कस्मिन्नु सर्वे संप्रतिष्ठिता भवन्तीति ।। १ ।।

atha hainaṁ sauryāyaṇī gārgyaḥ papraccha । *bhagavan etasmin puruṣe kāni svapanti? kāny asmiñjāgrati? katara eṣa devaḥ svapnān paśyati? kasyaitat sukhaṁ bhavati? kasmiṅ nu sarve saṁpratiṣṭhitā bhavanti iti* ।। 1 ।।

Then Gārgya, the son of Sūrya, asked Pippalāda: Venerable Sir, what are they that sleep in this *puruṣa* (person)? What are they that keep awake in him? Which one of the gods dreams? Whose is this happiness (*sukha*)? In whom are all these well-founded?

Seeker: All these questions are about *puruṣa*, the consciousness that feels pleasures and pains in its altering states. Is this *puruṣa* individual or cosmic?

Guru: *Prāṇa*, as we saw in the last chapter, functions both individually and cosmically, so too its ancillaries such as *prāṇa* and *apāna*. The knowing consciousness has also the same opposing facets of function, called *vyaṣṭi puruṣa* in the individual context and *samaṣṭi puruṣa* in the cosmic context. *Virāṭ puruṣa* is another name for the cosmic aspect of *puruṣa*, and literally means the person specifically luminous everywhere, the person in the form of everything specific, the person having the cosmic system for his body. As with *prāṇa*, the *puruṣa* of this stanza is the neutral one.

S: Is this neutral Consciousness subject to the three states the individual ones are subject to ?

G: It is rather difficult to answer this question for neutral Consciousness is beyond all conceptualisation. Yet it could be approached from a different perspective.

S: How?

G: The cosmic person (*virāṭ puruṣa*), as we envisage, is an expanded version of the individual person, with no characteristics left out. Each peculiarity in the individual person has therefore to be seen in its cosmic dimension in the *virāṭ puruṣa*. That the individual consciousness is subject to the altering states cf waking, dreaming and sleeping we are familiar with; the corresponding three states we postulate regarding the cosmic consciousness also.

S: Each one of us is aware of our altering states of consciousness. How can we think of the same with respect to the cosmic person?

G: You do have the direct experience of your own altering states; but can you experience or even think of, how I feel my own altering states?

S: No, apart from thinking of it as comparable to mine.

G: So too, none can have the direct experience or knowledge of the experiences of *virāṭ puruṣa*.

S: It sounds like a riddle — something exists, but we know nothing about it.

G: That is true. Life is the greatest of all such riddles; attempts are always made to solve these riddles.

S: Has any solution been suggested for the riddle of the altering states of *virāṭ puruṣa*?

G: Yes. The mythological explanation goes thus: The world is dissolved when the *virāṭ puruṣa* goes to sleep; and it is re-created when he wakes up; the world exists in between the two states as if in a dream. Another concept has the world emerging when the *virāṭ puruṣa*'s eyes are open when winking; and disappearing when he shuts his eyes. Another conception is that creation takes place when the day of the *virāṭ puruṣa* dawns and dissolution occurs at the close of the day. The time in between is the day time of Brahmā. These are all highly allegorical poetical images.

S: Poets have their own freedom to conceive such an imagery, but I don't understand the idea of the existence of the world as a dream of the *virāṭ puruṣa*.

G: You don't have to think of the dream of the *virāṭ puruṣa* to understand. In your case also, the world, supposedly directly perceived, is a dream.

S: How is that?

G: Are you, right now, fully awake or partly awake?

S: I am fully awake.

G: Suppose this dialogue goes on non-stop. Wouldn't you then feel fatigued and sleepy?

S: Of course I will.

G: Would you call it a waking state?

S: Yes.

G: Yet you would be sleepy. Can you be sure then that right now, in this waking state, there is no element of sleepiness?

S: I am not sure. May be there is a trace of sleepiness even now.

G: So too, on being awakened to new awareness one feels that till then one was in the dark, as far as that awareness was concerned. That means, even in the waking state, there is an element of darkness, of sleepiness. None have experienced the total waking state, except may be some great *yogī*. It is a state aspired to by all of us, but never attained. Now what about the state of sound sleep? Deep sleep is the state of knowing nothing. Any experience remembered is of 'something'. A state of experiencing nothing can never be recalled, something that none of us can claim to have experienced. Deep sleep is also thus a state not known to anyone, not remembered as having been experienced. The so-called sound sleep we claim to have had, is not the real deep-sleep, the real unknowing state.

S: It seems so.

G: Neither the *jāgrat* (waking state) nor the *suṣupti* (deep sleep) have thus been in anybody's experience, but are two extreme states which we all aspire to, our actual experience being something in between the two. What we call *svapna*, the dreaming state, is none other than this middle state. For this reason it is that *ṛṣis* regard this world and life in it as a lengthy dream. This experience, true for the individual person, must also be true of the cosmic person; the world is thus said to be a dream, dreamt by the *virāṭ-puruṣa*.

All these are our observations of the individual and cosmic aspects of the non-dual, neutral, transcendental Person, to whom these two aspects are related like the two sides of a coin. The transcendental *puruṣa* is thus the pure Unconditioned Consciousness which has inherent in it all the potential for the appearances of the three states of both the individual and cosmic *puruṣas*. The three states of the transcendental *puruṣa* are not apparent, as it itself is not apparent. What is apparent are only the *virāṭ-puruṣa* and the individual *puruṣa* and their three states.

S: Gārgya asked five questions as did Kausalya in the last chapter, and these two chapters form the two sides of the middle point of this Upaniṣad. Is this arrangement of any special significance?

G: It is just as well that you noticed this structural peculiarity of this Upaniṣad. These two central chapters and the five questions asked in each are somewhat like two brackets that enclose an unexpressed secret hinged on which the entire deliberation in this Upaniṣad moves. The *ṛṣi* leaves it to the seeker to discover and visualise this secret in his own intuitive mind. Indeed, what marks the glory of an Upaniṣad is that such ineffable secrets are left unexpressed.

S: Is it possible to make it clearer?

G: Having been left unexpressed even by the *ṛṣi*, how can we hope to express it in words? Yet we can try to have a closer look.

What was the central theme of the last chapter?

S: The origin and various functions of *prāṇa*?

G: Now what is Gārgya asking about in the present chapter?

S: About *puruṣa* and his various states.

G: Though conceivable distinctly, can these two, *prāṇa* and *puruṣa*, be isolated as entities?

S: Not at all. One does neither exist nor function without the other.

G: We may then say that existence and function of *prāṇa* and *puruṣa* are mutually dependent.

S: I think so.

G: Neither can be considered more real than the other. The indentity of the Real, intended to be conveyed to the seeker of penetrating vision is something mysterious hidden in between the two, bracketed by the two central chapters. Chapter III dealt with the origin and functions of *prāṇa*. Gārgya's questions in this chapter are about the various states of consciousness of *puruṣa*, the abode of all *prāṇa*s. What we are going to see in the forthcoming stanzas as the central principle in all these altering states, is a transcendental mind (*parā-manas*) whereas the central principle of the last chapter was *prāṇa*. The neutral principle which has *prāṇa*, the central principle of the last chapter, and the transcendental mind (*parā-manas*), the central principle of this chapter, for its two apparent facets is *puruṣa*. All these, along with the individual and cosmic aspects both of *prāṇa* and *puruṣa*, have to be correlated in an intuitive and mystical vision of non-duality.

S: Gārgya's questions go farther than the altering states of *puruṣa*. He wants to know also, whose is happiness, and in whom all are well-founded.

G: Yes. Life is always characterised by the quest for happiness, a peculiarity all the more dominant in human beings. Life is a constant search for happiness. It is achieved in the waking state through contact with objects that give pleasure, physical or mental. In the dream state, the objects enjoyed are creations of the very mind that enjoys them. The happiness experienced in deep-sleep is of a different order. One is aware of nothing in deep sleep, yet claims, on getting up, to have enjoyed a sound sleep. This soundness, though experienced while asleep, was not consciously felt then; it is therefore an unconscious experience of happiness. *Vedāntins* prefer to call it an experience of happiness veiled by the darkness of *avidyā* (ignorance). Gārgya's final question is concerning the ultimate basis of all these altering states and their respective experiences of happiness. The world *sarve* (all this) of the final question could, when looked at in the context of the theme of this chapter, be construed as referring to the states of consciousness and the happiness pertaining to each. However when looked at as part of the overall progression of thought in the Upaniṣad it could better be understood as suggesting everything covered so far in the previous chapters.

तस्मै स होवाच। यथा गार्ग्य मरीचयोऽर्कस्यास्तं गच्छतः सर्वा एतस्मिन् तेजोमण्डल एकीभवन्ति। ताः पुनः पुनरुदयतः प्रचरन्त्येवं ह वै तत् सर्वं परे देवे मनस्येकीभवति। तेन तर्ह्येष पुरुषो न शृणोति, न पश्यति, न जिघ्रति, न रसयते, न स्पृशते, नाभिवदते, नादत्ते, नानन्दयते, न विसृजते, नेयायते, स्वपितीत्याचक्षते ।। २ ।।

tasmai sa hovāca । *yathā gārgya marīcayo 'rkasyāstaṁ gacchataḥ sarvā estasmin tejo-maṇḍala ekī-bhavanti* । *tāḥ punaḥ punar udayataḥ pracaranty evaṁ ha vai tat sarvaṁ pare deve manasy ekī-bhavati* । *tena tarhy eṣa puruṣo na śṛṇoti, na paśyati, na jighrati, na rasayate, na spṛśate, nābhivadate, nādatte, nānandayate, na visṛjate, neyāyate, svapiti iti ācakṣate* ।। 2 ।।

To him then he said: O Gārgya, as all the rays of the setting sun become one with the orb of brilliances, and as they spread forth when he rises again and again, even so does all this becomes one with mind, the transcendental god.

The *puruṣa* in that state, therefore, hears not, sees not, smells not, tastes not, touches not, speaks not, takes not, rejoices not, emits not, moves not. It is therefore said, "He sleeps."

Seeker: Answering Gārgya's first question with the help of the sun analogy, it says all this becomes one with the 'mind'. Which mind is it? And whose mind is it?

Guru: Thought in each chapter moving around a key-concept, is one of the peculiarities of this Upaniṣad — the key concept in the present chapter is mind (*manas*), in the third chapter, *ātmā*, in the second *prāṇa*, in the first *prajāpati*. Instead of saying whose mind it is, it is said, *parā deva* (the transcendental god), *parā* meaning the transcendental, and *deva*, of the essence of brightness. This mind is thus a transcendental brightness. How do you conceive of *your own* mind?

S: As the faculty in me that thinks, imagines, loves, hates, gets emotionally moved and so on.

G: How do you conceive of *my* mind?

S: By likening it with what *my* mind means to *me*. There is no other way of thinking of someone else's mind.

G: Even so, the cosmic mind is to be conceived in the same manner. Thinking of the *puruṣa* we saw how the individual and cosmic aspects are merely two opposing facets of the non-dual *puruṣa*. The mind also is to be perceived likewise. The transcendental mind is the non-dual content which has the individual mind and the cosmic mind for its two facets like the two sides of a coin.

S: Is it equivalent to *Brahman*?

G: Not exactly. We could see the mind understood here as the sum total of the potential inherent in *Brahman* to think, imagine, dream and so on. Visualising what this transcendental mind is becomes all the more easy when *Brahman* is understood as of the essence of Consciousness (*cid-ghana*). Immense potential for numerous mental operations are inherent in one causal Consciousness. The sum total of such potential could be considered the transcendental mind as understood here.

S: What is the 'all this' that becomes one with the transcendental mind?

G: What can we distinctly see at night when all light is gone?

S: Nothing but darkness.

G: Likewise, what would you be able to perceive or conceive distinctly when mind ceases to function?

S: Nothing.

G: Whatever, then, is to be perceived externally or conceived internally, is therefore to be included in the 'all this'.

S: The *puruṣa* in that state is said to hear nothing, see nothing and so on. Does it mean that the senses and other faculties become non-functional?

G: It means even more. Not only do the senses and mental faculties stop functioning, even their objects, the so-called external world and its existence, become extinct, as it were, for the existence of the world is relevant only as and when it is known to someone's mind. The significance of the problem of whether this world exists, is when and where the faculty of knowing is functional. The cessation of hearing, seeing and so on is merely representative of the extinction of all, both subjective and objective.

S: The emergence of sun-beams at daybreak and their re-merging in the sun's orb at dusk though encountered daily, we know to be mere appearance; the sun continues to shine invisible to us. Is it true with the transcendental mind also? Is the merger of everything in the trancendental mind imaginary? The state of deep sleep also then must be understood as imaginary.

G: The transcendental mind and its altering states are what we are clarifying here with the sun-analogy as an aid. The apparent merger and re-emergence of sunlight, we know, is caused by the revolution of the earth around the sun; the sun always remains bright. So too is the transcendental mind. It never remains without function.

S: But the present analogy doesn't seem to suggest such an interpretation.

G: Such an interpretation is possible only when the approach is from the point of view of Reality, whereas the approach in the present analogy is from the point of view of appearance. What we finally arrive at is: It is the same transcendental mind that everything merges into and emerges out of.

S: How should we see it in the light of the sun-analogy?

G: The receding of sun-beams at dusk and their eventual disappearance along with the sun are part of our daily experience. Their being mere appearance in no way lessens its novelty.

So too with sunrise. Seeing the sudden gushing forth of bright beams from the fiery eastern horizon and the gradual emergence of the orb of the sun as if nudged out of a hole, is a breath-taking experience, ever new. Similar are our alternating experiences of deep sleep and wakefulness, though only apparent.

S: Here, what we are concerned with are not mere personal experiences; the experiences of the cosmic consciousness are also within our purview.

G: Surely.

S: The text refers to the deep sleep state only. How could this state be conceived as of the cosmic consciousness?

G: As the imaginary state in which all the multiple appearances merge with their own causal substance (*sat*). The religious concept of Deluge is a mythological version of the same, which in the Indian context is known as *pralaya*.

S: Is it not a great flood that submerges the entire world?

G: That is the allegory. The word *pralaya* literally only means 'proper dissolution', derived from *pra* for *prakarṣeṇa* meaning properly, and *laya*, dissolution.

S: Gārgya's first question was: What are they that sleep in this *puruṣa*? What is Pippalāda's direct answer to the question?

G: That the state in which everything — senses, mental faculties, their objects — goes back to and merges with the transcendental mind, in which all these sleep in the trancendental mind, is the *suṣupti* (deep-sleep) state of the *puruṣa*.

S: At least that mind should remain emergent then.

G: Yes, you are right, but it is the transcendental mind (*parā-manas*) of which we could neither think nor say anything. Functionless, it has no distinguishing characteristic, and no one is conscious of it. Shrouded by the darkness of *avidyā*, it is not known to anyone.

S: The happiness of sound sleep, as we saw in our discussions, is an experience unconsciously enjoyed, but the text here says, the *puruṣa* in this state 'rejoices not'. Why this disparity?

G: The happiness felt in deep sleep is that of the merger of the external factors of enjoyment into the *ānanda* content of the self. Having no conditioning factor, this *ānanda* experience remains hidden even to the consciousness that experiences it. The reference in the text to 'rejoices not' indicates this lack of awareness of enjoyment.

S: The state in which everything merges in the transcendental mind was seen as *suṣupti*. How does it differ from *turīya*?

G: *Suṣupti* is the state in which everything merges in causal consciousness that is unconscious of itself; *turīya* is the experience in which everything merges in the causal consciousness with full self-awareness. In *suṣupti* the merger of everything is in total darkness; in *turīya* the merger is in total brightness — the *parā-manas* (transcendental mind) of this stanza. It is in this *parā-manas* that everything is well-founded. The answer to the first question of Gārgya happens to be thus the answer to his final question as well. The other three questions will be answered in the stanzas coming up, with this *parā-manas* for firm basis.

> प्राणाग्नय एवैतस्मिन् पुरे जाग्रति। गार्हपत्यो ह वा एषोऽपानो व्यानोऽन्वाहार्यपचनो यद्गार्हपत्यात् प्रणीयते प्रणयनादाहवनीयः प्राणः ॥ ३ ॥
>
> *prāṇāgnaya evaitasmin pure jāgrati । gārhapatyo ha vā eṣo'pāno vyāno'nvāhārya-pacano yad gārhapatyāt praṇīyate praṇayanād āhavanīyaḥ prāṇaḥ* ॥ 3 ॥

> The fires of *prāṇa* indeed are wakeful in this city (*pura*). Of them, *apāna* is the householder's fire (*gārhapatyāgni*), *vyāna* the southern sacrificial fire (*anvāhārya-pacana*). *Prāṇa*, called so because it is kindled (*praṇayanāt*) from *gārhapatyāgni*, is the *āhavanīyāgni*.

Seeker: This is answer to Gārgya's second question. Which is the city (*pura*) referred to?

Guru: How the *puruṣa*, when all his faculties cease to function, individually as well as cosmically, is thought of as fully alseep, was considered in the last stanza. *Puruṣa* literally means one who reposes or sleeps in a city (*pura*); the *pura* therefore is the city in which *puruṣa* rests.

S: Each of us being an individual person, couldn't we consider our own body as this city?

G: Yes, we should. Some scriptures, like the *Bhagavad Gītā* refer to this body as a city of nine gates.

S: The world should then be the city in which the cosmic *puruṣa* rests.

G: Yes, you are right.

S: The *prāṇa*s alone are taken into account here as keeping the *puruṣa* awake. Why are factors like the senses and mind, also functioning in the waking state, overlooked here?

G: These *prāṇa*s are to be seen in the light of and as a sequel to their functions described in the last chapter. We have seen how none of the bodily, sense and mental functions are excluded from those of *prāṇa*s. It is better you refer back to them once more than repeating it here. All such functions of *prāṇa*s are likened to blazing sacrificial fires.

S: What is the relevance of sacrificial fire here?

G: *Yajña* or sacrificial offering, one of the most significant concepts of the Vedic culture, varies in its philosophical implications as the context demands. Its relevance here derives from its bringing together the individual and cosmic aspects of existence.

S: Could you please clarify it?

G: Who is the performer of the *yajña* you are familiar with?

S : Human beings like us.

G: What is their goal?

S: Obtaining the favour and blessings of the gods.

G: Don't you know that each god represents some universal phenomenon of nature?

S: Yes, I do.

G: What do we know of these phenomena?

S: Nothing, apart from certain facts known to modern science.

G: What do we know of ourselves, the individuals who make these offerings?

S: Virtually nothing.

G: Ignorant though we are of ourselves, we aspire always for happiness in this world we are ignorant of.

S: It looks so.

G: Yet, that the actualisation of this happiness is not in our control is our experience. Why is it so?

S: May be because we know neither ourselves, the aspirants to happiness, nor the world that we regard as the source of happiness.

G: A discord thus exists between our aspiration and the possibility of attaining it. This discord is the cause of all unrest in us. The ancient seers of India discovered a way out; they called it *yajña*.

S: How does it save us?

G: How it saves us, what is the philosophy and psychology behind the concept of *yajña*, all these we have discussed in detail under the Peace Invocation in the beginning.

We are ignorant of ourselves, of the world, of the one Reality underlying everything, though we are all part of It, one with It — part of nature, and one with nature. Our ignorance in no way affects our oneness with nature or Reality. Reflecting on this oneness reveals that our existence, our desire for happienss, all our efforts to actualise it, are one with the one Reality, are its integral parts, are its self-expressions. Ideas formulated owing to our own ignorance, as part of our existence, aspirations, and our efforts — are all illusory. This revelation forces us to give back to nature whatever has been thought of as 'I' and 'mine'. This giving back is the *yajña* we have discussed before. Our ignorance, makes us think of ourselves and the objects of happiness as entities existing separately, and results in the notion that the object or the world out there is 'mine', as the object of my knowledge, the object of my enjoyment. It is this sense of 'I' and 'mine' that creates the need to offer ourselves back to the total. Rid of ignorance and the resultant 'I'-'mine', one realises the lack of meaning of actual ritual offering. This is the kind of sacrificial fire conceived as awake in the *puruṣa*.

S: Why is *gārhapatyāgni* equated to *apāna* of the *puruṣa?*

S: *Apāna* is seated in the organs of excretion and procreation (see III. 5 above) and its presiding deity is the Earth (III.8). Excretion represents the disappearance of a prior form of appearance, and procreation the emergence of a new form of appearance, both together thus signify the never-ceasing process of manifestation taking place both individually and cosmically.

Gārhapatya means that which is related to a householder's life, and *agni* means fire. A householder who adheres to the ritualitstic tradition of the Vedas is bound to keep in the house a sacrificial fire constantly alive in its circular pit. Considering the household as the previously mentioned *pura* (city), this *gārhapatyāgni* is the *puruṣa* reposing therein. The unceasing becoming of excretion and procreation, are the functions of *apāna*, and just as *apāna* is always alive in a living body, so too *gārhapatyāgni* is always alive in the household.

S: *Udāna* was seen (III.6) as seated in the circulatory and nervous systems. How is it equivalent to *anvāhārya pacana*?

G: Different sacrificial fires are customaritly kindled by Vedic ritualists.

S: All fire is fire. How can it be different in kind?

G: The difference is only in the area of the household where the fire is kindled and the time of kindling.

S: Where and when are the different fires kindled?

G: *Gārhapatyāgni* is to be permanently kept alive. *Anvāhārya pacana*, also known as *dakṣiṇāgni*, is kindled in the southern part of the household when offerings are made to the departed. The fire made for making offerings to gods is known as *āhavanīyāgni*. *Gārhapatyāgni*, the central fire, is the one from which all the other fires are to be kindled.

S: How is *anvāhārya pacana* comparable to the circulatory and nervous systems of the body?

G: *Vyāna*'s funtion is to reach vitality to every part of the body through the endlessly branched circulatory and nervous systems. Our ancestors also similarly branched off, the father and mother who are our own progenitors also had between them two fathers and two mothers, and four in the generation prior to theirs, branching off thus endlessly. The fire kindled to make offerings for the ancestors, for this reason, also is supposed to branch off endlessly so that the offerings reach each ancestor, a function comparable to *vyāna*'s.

S: How is *prāṇa* comparable to *āhavanīyāgni*?

G: *Prāṇa* is the vitality which energises senses, the outlets of consciousness, often referred to as gods, and for this reason the fire kindled to make offerings to the gods is *prāṇa*-like. *Āhavanīyāgni* we know is kindled, as are other fires, from *gārhapatyāgni*. The act of kindling fire is called *praṇayana*. *Āhavanīyāgni* gained the name *prāṇa* because of its *praṇayana* (being kindled) from *gārhapatyāgni*, even as the subsidiary *prāṇa* is derived from the chief *prāṇa*.

S: The word *prāṇa* it seems is used in this Upaniṣad in varying senses.

G: Yes. It is one of the important points to be kept in mind while going through the chapters of this Upaniṣad. The *prāṇa* of the first chapter was the animating principle in each being. It was divided into five distinct functions in the next chapter, each one of the subdivisions was still called *prāṇa*. This latter *prāṇa* is here equated to the *āhavanīyāgni* where even the similarity with the word *praṇayana* is counted.

यदुच्छ्वासनिःश्वासावेतावाहुती समं नयतीति स समानः। मनो ह वाव यजमान इष्टफलमेवोदानः स एनं यजमानमहरहर्ब्रह्म गमयति ।। ४ ।।

yad ucchvāsa-niḥśvāsāv etāv āhutī samaṁ nayatīti sa samānaḥ । *mano ha vāva yajamāna, iṣṭa-phalam evodānaḥ sa enaṁ yajamānam ahar ahar brahma gamayati* ।। 4 ।।

As the one who keeps the two oblations of breathing in and breathing out in perfect balance, he is called *samāna*. The sacrificer is but the mind. *Udāna* is the favourable result attained.

He (*udāna*) conducts him (the mind) to *Brahman* day after day.

Seeker: How can breathing in and breathing out be sacrificial oblations (*āhuti*)?

Guru: *Āhuti* is the act of offering something in a fire sacrifice. How the life of one who knows himself is transformed into a *yajña* we have already dealt with in detail. The function of the respiratory system, the sign of life, is perfect when breathing in and breathing out are well balanced, the two together therefore stand for the individual who makes an offering of himself.

S: How does *samāna* keep the two breaths in balance?

G: That *samāna* seated in the middle of the body keeps the body in perfect balance by distributing nourishment equitably (III.3), and, seated in between the earth and the sun, maintains the balance between the two (III.8), we have already seen. What concerns us here is the perfectly balanced existence of *puruṣa* in the the waking state where in-breath and out-breath find themselves well balanced, or they are brought to balance through practices like *prāṇāyāma*. Effecting such a balanced existence is considered as an offering made to the total system of existence, and is called *samāna* again.

S: Why is mind treated as the sacrificer?

G: *Yajamāna* (sacrificer) is the one for whose sake *yajña* is performed, the one who pays for it. A special seat in the hall is allotted to him and his wife. Only in the wakeful state are we capable of controlling our physical and mental functions and this is always done by our mind which decides what is beneficial and what is not, what is right and what wrong, in effect, what sort of balance is most suitable. Mind is thus the measurer of the *yajña* as the word *yajamāna* itself indicates, where *yaja* stands for *yajña* and *māna* means measuring rod.

S: What is common in the fovourable result of rituals and the function of *udāna*?

G: *Udāna*'s function is to give us our orientation towards higher values in life (III.7). As for *yajñas*, they are also motivated by the hope of attaining something higher, and therefore *udāna* is likened to the favourable results expected of a sacrifice.

Prāṇa, *apāna*, *vyāna*, *samāna* and *udāna*, the five distinct functions of the chief *prāṇa*, are thus brought into the waking state as controlling its various aspects, while treating the whole situation as a fire sacrifice.

S: How is mind, the sacrificer, conducted by *udāna* to *Brahman* day after day?

G: Right now we are concerned with the waking state of *puruṣa*, the only state we have any control over. On treating all our activities in the waking state as a *yajña* and controlling them accordingly, what will then be our view about ourselves?

S: We'll see ourselves as existing and functioning as an integral part of the total existence; all our actitivies will be directed so as to be an oblation offered in the fire of total existence.

G: Even such an understanding is possible only in our waking state; the other states are beyond our control. Seeing one's own life as a *yajña* is therefore an experience of the waking state, an experience of seeing all varieties of its functions including those of other states, as various modes of expression of the one and only Consciousness. The plenitude of this one Consciousness is what is known as *Brahman*, the Absolute. The same Consciousness functions as the sacrificer, the mind, and also as its aspirations for benefits. Once the sacrificer becomes aware of his oneness with the Absolute, he sees the planitude of the Absolute in himself, in his aspirations, and in the efforts to accomplish them. No matter what activity the mind (the sacrificer) is engaged in, it sees all of them only as various conditioned modes of the one unconditioned Consciousness. The zenith of the higher values aspired to by the human mind is the function of *udāna*. Put figuratively, *udāna* leads *manas* (mind, the sacrificer) to the attainment of *Brahman* in and through every instance of the day-to-day affairs of life.

Suṣupti and *jāgrat* are the two states we have been examining so far in this chapter — the former is the state of knowing nothing, even of ourselves, and the latter the state of knowing everything. These are the extremes between which our consciousness moves. Knowing this consciousness in all its plenitude is the essence of *Brahma-jñāna*, the wisdom of the Absolute. Penetrating the states of individual consciousness, as if by a leap, takes us to the wisdom of *Brahman*, to the attainment of *Brahman*. This sudden shift in the dimension of what is being speculated on and its repercussions on our intuitive vision of what is real are ineffable. However it becomes transparent to us leaving no trace of vagueness in our intuitive inlook. It is a secret that cannot be conveyed through words, hidden between the lines of the Upaniṣads, true to its literal meaning of 'the secret teaching'. It is because of this that familiarity with the texts and commentaries of the Upaniṣads does not make one a *jñānin*.

A total revaluation of the concept of *yajña* is another feat accomplished here.

S: How is it?

G: The *yajamāna* performs a *yajña*, desiring the attainment of some goal, usually of worldly value. But in the new kind of sacrifice portrayed here where mind is the *yajamāna* and *udāna* the force leading to its benefit, the final goal attained is no less than the wisdom of *Brahman*, the attainment of *Brahman*, the most ultimate of all the goals man can ever aspire for. Such is the value shift that occurs to *yajña* when it transcends Vedic ritualism to the reach of Vedāntic wisdom.

अत्रैष देवः स्वप्ने महिमानमनुभवति। यद् दृष्टं दृष्टमनुपश्यति; श्रुतं श्रुतमेवार्थमनुशृणोति; देशदिगन्तरैश्च प्रत्यनुभूतं पुनः पुनः प्रत्यनुभवति; दृष्टं चादृष्टं च, श्रुतं चाश्रुतं चानुभूतं चाननुभूतं च, सच्चासच्च, सर्वं पश्यति सर्वः पश्यति ।। ५ ।।

atraiṣa devaḥ svapne mahimānam anubhavati । *yad dṛṣṭaṁ dṛṣṭam anupaśyati; śrutaṁ śrutam evārtham anuśṛṇoti; deśa-digantaraiś ca praty anubhūtaṁ punaḥ punaḥ praty anubhavati; dṛṣṭaṁ ca adṛṣṭaṁ ca, śrutaṁ cāśrutaṁ cānubhūtaṁ cānanubhūtaṁ ca, sac cāsac ca, sarvaṁ paśyati sarvaḥ paśyati* ।। 5 ।।

This god here in the dreaming state experiences (its own) greatness, for he sees again what had once been seen, for he hears again what had once been heard, for

> he experiences again what had once been experienced repeatedly at various places in different directions. What has been seen and not seen, what has been heard and not heard, what has been experienced and not experienced, what is existent and non-existent — he sees everything, as everything.

Seeker: Who is the 'this god' (*esaḥ devaḥ*) mentioned here?

Guru: We, in the preceding stanzas, were thinking of a transcendental mind or god. This stanza continues the same line of thought and so the same mind is referred to here as ' this god'.

S: 'This god' is said to experience its own greatness in its dreaming state. The other two states were not stated to have any such glory. Why is it so?

G: That neither the fully waking state nor complete deep sleep is actually experienced by anyone has already been made clear. All actual experiences thus form part of a lengthy dream, or rather to experience a dream-world is the greatness of the transcendental mind.

S: The states of consciousness are usually discussed in the order *jāgrat*, *svapna* and *suṣupti*, but here it goes the other way—*suṣupti, jāgrat* and *svapna*. Is this alteration due to the above fact?

G: It is to be presumed so.

S: Whose dream is it?

G: It should be of the transcendental mind. We, the world we are in, and all our experiences are but a dream dreamt by this transcendental mind. It is something our mind, a mere speck of that vast dream, is incapable of grasping and imagining, except as a great wonder.

S: How could *svapna* or dream be defined?

G: Dreams vary. Some are very pleasant; some are sheer mightmare. In dreams we experience seeing many things, hearing many things, tasting many things and so on, the concerned sense-organs remaining non-functioning, while the dreaming mind plays their role. All the objects experienced have mind alone for their source; those objects are also enjoyed by the very same mind. Dream could therefore be defined as the state in which both subject and object arise from mind, wherein the subject also enjoys the object. Śaṅkara puts the same in another fashion by saying that dream is the state in which senses merge with mind, while the mind remains itself not merged with anything.

S: It is the case of our personal dreams. How can we explain the cosmic dream we call the world?

G: What is the one underlying Reality in all that is apprent as the world?

S: It is *Brahman*, as the Upaniṣads teach.

G: Is it not *Brahman* that we call *ātmā* in the capacity of being the underlying reality in each of us?

S: Yes, of course.

G: What we call the world, as Vedānta teaches, is merely the aggregate of apparent forms this one Reality assumes, without itself undergoing any intrinsic change. What is this Reality in essence?

S: It is pure Consciousness alone.

G: One or many?

S: One alone.

G: Then it must be this one Consciousness, in its dream, that assumes the multiple forms of this world, of the knowers and enjoyers and also of the experience of enjoying. Personal dreams are short-lived while the cosmic dream is a lengthy one. Both are realised as being mere dreams only on waking up. The potential of this world-dream inherent in pure Consciousness is its greatness (*mahimā*).

S: Why is this potential a great one?

G: In dreams it is one mind that unfolds itself as the perceiver, the object perceived and perception. Does it need any external help to accomplish this?

S: No. Perhaps the incipient memory factors (*vāsanās*) and the hopes and aspirations in the mind might have some role, yet everything happens within mind, impelled by nothing external.

G: We do not know how it happens or, why it happens. It is a mystery, a sign of the greatness of the transcendental mind.

S: Dream is not the only state in which mind unfolds itself as everything. All the three states, their experiences and the objects experienced, according to Vedānta, are all various forms assumed by one Consciousness, the one Reality.

G: You are right. The one Reality, Consciousness in essenece, is self-effulgent. Unceasingly altering forms are assumed by it, illumined by it and in it, which we call the world. None of these exists apart from the one Reality, even as no dream exists apart from the dreaming mind; the only difference is that to understand the world as a dream needs a contemplatively penetrating mind; to understand an ordinary dream as the mind's creation is easier. The self-expressing greatness is the same in both.

S: The text says, he sees again what had ever been seen, he hears again what had ever been heard and so on. Past experiences, we know, play a major role in shaping our dreams. This statement, according to certain commentators, refers to one's experiences in previous incarnations. What do you think of it?

S: Such notions are relevant only when we think of the continuance of the cosmic dream. Even in personal dreams, though much influenced by our past experiences, we are not sure how such experiences shape our dreams. As to the continuance of the cosmic dream, though genetics partly explains the mechanical side of the transmission of information from generation to generation, it still remains the mysterious greatness of the Real, the one Consciousness, the *parā-manas*.

S: Why is it said, he sees what has been seen and not seen, he hears what has been heard and not heard, and so on, as if it is a puzzle?

G: Really both the personal dreams and the cosmic dream, the world, are puzzles. The more we try to understand them the more mysterious they turn. Still our personal dreams are not mere re-enacting of our past experiences. Our hopes, aspirations, anxieties, fears, all appear to us in our dreams. So too unexpected and inexplicable phenomena appear in the cosmic dream called the world, as though they are the expressions of the hopes, anxieties and fears hidden in the cosmic mind. As the potential hidden in Reality remains unknown always, no one can predict what is probable and improbable in the world.

स यदा तेजसाभिभूतो भवति, अत्रैष देवः स्वप्नान् न पश्यत्यथ तदैतस्मिञ्छरीरे एतत्सुखं भवति ।। ६ ।।

sa yadā tejasābhibhūto bhavati, atraiṣa devaḥ svapnān na paśyaty atha tadaitasmin śarīre etat sukhaṁ bhavati || 6 ||

Overcome with brilliance (*tejas*) this god (mind) then sees no dream. Confined thus to the concerned body arise pleasure (and pain).

Seeker: Are the pleasure and pain that of the dreaming state?

Guru: Answering the fourth question of Gārgya, this stanza concerns itself with the pleasures and pains one has in all the three states. The three occur to the transcendental mind and the respective pleasures and pains are also experienced by the same mind.

S: Only the dreaming state is directly referred to in this stanza and that too in the negative sense.

G: You are right. When experiencing the pleasures and pains of what we call the three states, we are oblivious of the reality that they are all part of a lengthy dream. Instead of seeing them as part of a dream dreamt by the transcendental mind, one thinks one is experiencing it personally.

S: We are used to taking what we see while awake as real and what is seen in dreams as unreal. Here we don't see any such discrimination.

G: That is true. When awake what you see in that state is real and dreams are taken to be unreal. Not conscious of a world experienced while awake, in the dreaming state one takes what is dreamt as real; its unreality becomes evident only on waking. So too the wakeful world becomes unreal when the waking state gives way to dream or deep-sleep. The world seen as real in one state is thus unreal for the other states. Always altering in states, consciousness moves from one real world to another real world, or from one unreal world to another unreal world. No world experienced is absolutely real; what is absolutely real is one transcendent mind alone, which, through its altering states, experiences all these illusory worlds of pleasure and pain.

S: Which is the body confined to which the mind experiences pleasures and pains?

G: Advaita Vedānta, after Śaṅkara, had developed the idea of a gross body (*sthūla śarīra*) identified with which the self enjoys external objects in the waking state, a subtle body (*sūkṣma śarīra*) with which the self enjoys dreams, and a causal body (*kāraṇa śarīra*) with which the self experiences the unconscious pleasure of sound sleep. But no such reference to these bodies is seen in any of the basic scriptures; only their commentaries have brought in such ideas. Having seen what we call the three states as parts of a lengthy dream, the problem of whether such bodies exist does not bother us.

S: What then is the relevance of the reference to body here?

G: The original word for body is *śarīra*, meaning that which perishes. The transcendent mind, the Pure Consciousness, is the imperishable Reality, but it becomes subject to incessant conditioning making apparent the constantly altering states and the concerned experiences. Such conditioning factors, momentary by themselves, are here named *śarīra* which includes in it everything conceivable from the grossest physical elements to the subtlest animating principle in us.

S: Why can't we classify these conditioning factors as the above-mentioned three *śarīra*s?

G: Treating the conditioning factors as bodies gives the impression that they have their own existence apart from the one Reality, a stand unacceptable to Vadānta. Given the oneness of Reality, whatever conditioning it becomes subject to has to be some apparent manifest form of the same Reality. This Reality being Pure Consciousness in essence, the conditioning factors should be the different ways in which it shines. Hence, if at all any classification of the conditioning factors is needed, it should be something like the gross manifestation of consciousness (*sthūla bhāna*), the subtle manifestation of consciousness (*sūkṣma bhāna*), the causal manifestaion of consciousness (*kāraṇa bhāna*), as Narayana Guru does in his *Daraśana-Mālā*. So conditioned, Pure Consciousness assumes the forms of the knower, the known and knowledge, of the doer of deeds and the deeds done, of the enjoyer, the enjoyed and enjoyment. Beyond all these variegated experiences is the awareness that all this takes place in one Consciousness, in the Self, in oneself — the unconditioned Self-awareness which goes together with the unconditioned Self-contentment (*ātmānanda*), the Supreme Happiness (*paramānanda*) aimed at by all Vedānta. This blissfulness is often called *turīya*, literally 'the fourth' as related to the three states already discussed.

S: Given that no reference to suffering is made in the text of this stanza, why can't we take the happiness of this stanza as this *turīya* itself?

G: The reference to experiencing pleasure confined to body stands against such an interpretation. *Turīya*, the transcendental awareness of non-duality, which cannot be related as 'this' or 'that' is beyond all bodily experiences.

S: One more point needs clarification: There is reference to a brilliance that overcomes mind, resulting in not seeing the world as a dream. What brilliance is this? Is it related to *taijasa*, the aspect of self that enjoys dreams?

G: The *Māṇḍūkya Upaniṣad* names the consciousness in its dreaming state *taijasa*. The *tejas* (brilliance or brightness) of the present text is the knower and enjoyer of the cosmic dream called the world. The infatuation with the desire for pleasure is a sort of dazzling brightness that shrouds the fact that this very desire is merely part of a dream. Unable to see the real, mind does not see dream as dream.

The situation as a whole, taking into account all the states of consciousness could be represented graphically as shown below:

> The three states of *suṣupti*, *jāgrat*, and *svapna* could be seen as forming the vertical axis, with the former two, the never-actualised states, for its extreme poles. No knower or enjoyer is relevant to an unactualised experience, so they are meaningful only in the dreaming state. The mind that functions as the knower and the enjoyer has in it the potential to create the objects to be known and enjoyed also. Action thus takes place in that realm resulting in the appearance of the transactional world called *vyāvahārika loka*.

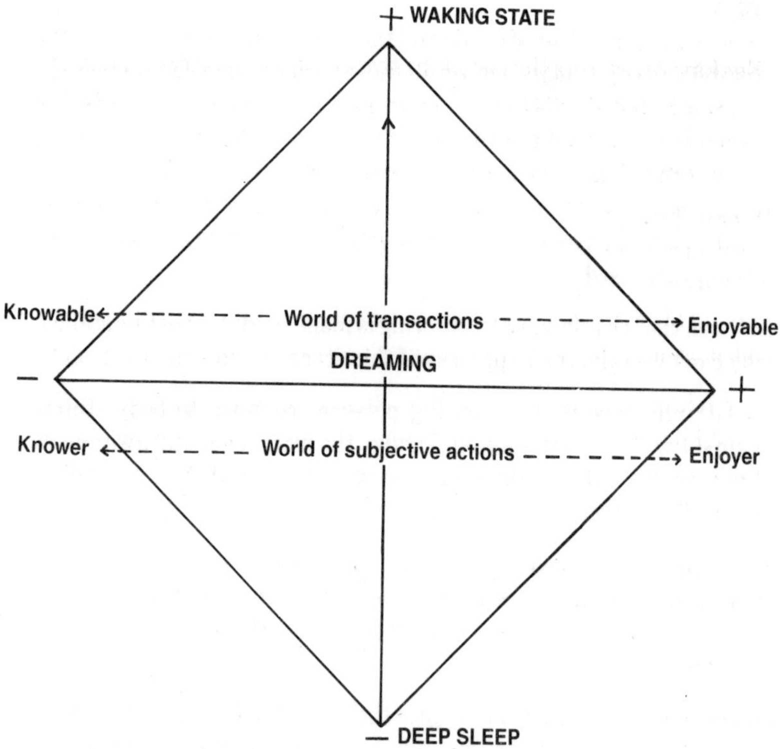

The horizontal plane could come across the vertical exis at any level. The knower-enjoyer distinction as well as the function of mind attenuates and finally vanishes at the two extremes of the waking state and complete deep-sleep. The god called mind, depicted in Stanzas 2 to 6 of this chapter, is thus to be seen as pertaining to such a structurally perfect functional whole.

स यथा सोम्य वयांसि वासोवृक्षं संप्रतिष्ठन्ते, एवं ह वै तत् सर्वं पर आत्मनि संप्रतिष्ठते ।। ७ ।।

sa yathā somya vayāṁsi vāso-vr̥kṣaṁ saṁpratiṣṭhante, evaṁ ha vai tat sarvaṁ para ātmani saṁpratiṣṭhate ।। 7 ।।

Even as birds, O Dear, have trees for their dwelling, so does everything here have the transcendental Self for a dwelling.

Seeker: Answering the last of the five questions of Gārgya, Pippalāda says, the transcendental Self is that in which all is well founded. Is there any implied meaning in comparing the world and its abode, to birds and a tree.

Guru: Tree remains motionless, but the birds that rest on it move out in all directions and find enjoyment, but at dusk return to the same tree. So too are we. Whatever be the worlds of enjoyment we move around in, we are always well founded in the one Reality, the Self Supreme; we have no other refuge than the Reality in us.

It is impossible to predict which directions the birds will fly into and what kind of enjoyment they will find. Still the centre of attraction and final refuge of the birds will remain the tree. Likewise, nothing in our life is predictable. Life advances through its altering states of *suṣupti*, *jāgrat* and *svapna* with all its variegated yet unpredictable experiences. Still none of these experiences goes beyond the bounds of the transcendental Self.

It is in a horizontal direction that the birds fly off from the tree and wander around, and the tree always remains vertical and motionless. So too, the one Reality that is the abode of all activities, while spreading out horizontally in life, is changeless and motionless, as though standing vertically.

S: The birds, while they take refuge in the tree at dusk, keep up their individuality. What is comparable in human life in that respect?

G: Man, to be fully happy, while living with the awareness of his oneness with Reality, should live as an indidvidual, aware of all the personal traits in him as part of nature with enough opportunities available to express himself to his full satisfaction. It is what makes life meaningul; it is the final liberation man can aspire for.

S: Do the *ātmā* of Chapter III and the *parā ātmā* of this chapter mean the same thing?

G: They are of the same meaning but in the *parā ātmā* the meaning attains its ultimate limit as the one Reality in which everything apparent abides. The third chapter showed *ātmā* simply as the source of *prāṇa*. We get a detailed picture of everything that dwells in the *parā ātmā* in the next stanza. From now on all discussions in this Upaniṣad will revolve around this *parā ātmā*.

पृथिवी च पृथिवीमात्रा चापश्चापोमात्रा च, तेजश्च तेजोमात्रा च, वायुश्च वायुमात्रा चाकाशश्चाकाशमात्रा च, चक्षुश्च द्रष्टव्यं च, श्रोत्रं च श्रोतव्यं च, घ्राणं च घ्रातव्यं च, रसश्च रसयितव्यं च, त्वक्च स्पर्शयितव्यं च, वाक्च वक्तव्यं च, हस्तौ चादातव्यं चोपस्थश्चानन्दयितव्यं च, पायुश्च विसर्जयितव्यं च, पादौ च गन्तव्यं च, मनश्च मन्तव्यं च, बुद्धिश्च बोद्धव्यं चाहंकारश्चाहंकर्तव्यं च, चित्तं च चेतयितव्यं च, तेजश्च विद्योतयितव्यं च, प्राणश्च विधारयितव्यं च ॥ ८ ॥

pr̥thivī ca pr̥thivī-mātrā ca āpaś cāpo-mātrā ca, tejas ca tejo-mātrā ca, vāyuś ca vāyu-mātrā ca ākāśaś cākāśa-mātrā ca, cakṣuś ca draṣṭavyaṁ ca, śrotraṁ ca śrotavyaṁ ca, ghrāṇaṁ ca ghrātavyaṁ ca, rasaś ca rasayitavyaṁ ca, tvak ca sparśayitavyaṁ ca vāk ca vaktavyaṁ ca, hastau cādātavyaṁ ca upasthaś cānandayitavyaṁ ca, pāyuś ca visarjayitavyaṁ ca, pādau ca gantavyaṁ ca, manaś ca mantavyaṁ ca, buddhiś ca boddhavyaṁ ca ahaṁkāraś cāhaṁ-kartavyaṁ ca, cittaṁ ca cetayitavyaṁ ca, tejaś ca vidyotayitavyaṁ ca, prāṇaś ca vidhārayitavyaṁ ca ॥ 8 ॥

The gross element earth and its subtle aspect, the gross element water and its subtle aspect, the gross element fire and its subtle aspect, the gross element air and its subtle aspect, the gross element space and its subtle aspect, sight and what can be seen, hearing and what can be heard, smell and what can be smelled, taste and what can be tasted, touch and what can be touched, speech and what can be spoken, hands and what can be handled, genitals and what can be enjoyed, organ of defecation and what can be defecated, feet and what can be walked to, mind and what can mind be applied on, intellect and what can be conceived, the 'I' sense and what can be sensed as 'I', memory factor and what can be memorised, effulgence and what can be illumined, *prāṇa* and what can be supported by it

— all these have the transcendental Self for their dwelling.

Seeker: This stanza delineates all aspects of existence as having the one Self for dwelling. Is there any order to this portrayal?

Guru: Yes, of course. It begins with the grossest and the most inert of all forms of existence, earth, and ends with *prāṇa* the life principle, next only to *ātmā*. The five physical elements in their order of grossness are mentioned first, each having its own gross and visible aspect, and invisible and subtle aspect. The physical earth we perceive, for instance, is the gross (*sthūla*) aspect, which is blended with traces of the other four elements. Pure earth, with no blend of any other element, is the subtle aspect, which is imperceptible. So too with the other four elements. The gross form of elements blended with traces of other elements, is known as *sthūla bhūta*, and the way of blending is called *pañcīkaraṇa*, literally quintuplication. The gross element for this reason is sometimes call *pañcīkṛta bhūta* (the quintupled element) and the pure and the subtle ones, *apañcīkṛta bhūta* (unquintupled element), otherwise known as *mātrā* or *tanmātrā* (the thing pure and simple).

All these have bearing on the physical aspect of existence, individual as well as cosmic. Then comes the listing of our sense-organs and their objects. While the former are part of our individual beingness, the latter belong to the cosmic system, each a quality of the five basic elements: smell is the quality of earth, taste of water, form of fire, touch of air, sound of space. Senses and their objects, thus belong to a realm where individual faculties and cosmic factors interact within a non-dual whole.

Then comes reference to organs of action whose field of activity is much limited compared to that of senses. Their role is ensuring active endurance of individual organisms. Mental faculties, more interior in nature, four in number, called *antaḥ-karaṇa*s, are mentioned then along with their objects. Then comes the still internal factor *tejas* (effulgence) and all that is illumined by it. Behind the *tejas* is the vitalising principle *prāṇa* whose source is *ātmā* itself. That *ātmā*, in which dwells everything, from the grossest physical elements to the subtlest *prāṇa*, is the Reality finally visualised.

S: Each of the items mentioned here is paired with its counterpart. Is it an intentional peculiarity of expression, and if so, what is the intention?

G: It is intentional. Conceiving anything always implies along with it its opposite, though not noticed by us. The idea of bigness implies smallness. The notion of father has implicit in it the idea of children. Grossness implies subtlety. Senses have their objects as their counterparts, and subject has object. One limb in every such pair is meaningless without the other, and both together constitute a functional life situation. All such situations emamate from the one source, *ātmā*.

> **एष हि द्रष्टा स्प्रष्टा श्रोता घ्राता रसयिता मन्ता बोद्धा कर्ता विज्ञानात्मा पुरुषः। स परेऽक्षरे आत्मनि सम्प्रतिष्ठते ।। ९ ।।**
>
> *eṣa hi draṣṭā spraṣṭā śrotā ghrātā rasayitā mantā boddhā kartā vijñānātmā puruṣaḥ* । *sa pare'kṣare ātmani sampratiṣṭhate* ।। 9 ।।
>
> He verily is the *puruṣa*, the seer, the one who touches, the hearer, the smeller, the taster, the perceiver, the knower, the doer, the specifically knowing self. He is well seated in the Transcendental, undecaying Self.

Seeker: All that could be conceived in this world was included in the listing of the last stanza. Why is a new list needed, equating every item in it with *puruṣa*?

Guru: It elaborates the answer to Gārgya's final question. All the items included in the last stanza, as a closer look at it reveals, pertain to the visible world.

S: How can factors such as mental faculties and inner effulgence and *prāṇa* be treated as part of the visible world?

G: The 'visible world' does not simply mean the world seen with our eyes. All faculties of perception including mind constituting the 'eye' that sees, everything perceivable and conceivable is included in the 'visible world', the *prāṇa*, *tejas*, and so on of the last stanza not excluded.

S: Who is then the perceiver of that 'visible world'?

G: That is the point clarified in this stanza. The *puruṣa* is this perceiver.

S: Why is this perceiver called *puruṣa*?

G: The word *puruṣa*, you know, means the dweller in the city. Everything portrayed in the last verse together constitutes the present city. It is to this *puruṣa*, the consciousness that pervades and encompasses the whole of this city, that the alterting states of consciousness and the concerned experiences of pleasure and pain occur.

S: The Sāṁkhya system admits the dual realities of *prakṛti* and *puruṣa*. Can't we take what was described in the last verse as *prakṛti* and in the present one as *puruṣa*?

G: To look at it that way is not wrong, but will not do full justice to the Upaniṣadic vision?

S: How?

G: Treating *prakṛti* and *puruṣa* as two distinct realities, as the Sāṁkhyans do, does not admit a non-dual Self. The Upaniṣad here, while portraying the *prakṛti* aspect in the last stanza and the *puruṣa* aspect in the present one, visualises both as having *ātmā* for their common abode. *Ātmā* pervades the whole of these *prakṛti* and *puruṣa* aspects, like gold pervades all ornaments, and all together exists as a functional, indivisible, living whole. Scriptures like the *Bhagavad Gītā* also sometimes prefer to portray the non-dual Self on this Sāṁkhyan grounding.

परमेवाक्षरं प्रतिपद्यते, स यो ह वै तदच्छायमशरीरमलोहितं शुभ्रमक्षरं वेदयते; यस्तु सोम्य, स सर्वज्ञः सर्वो भवति, तदेष श्लोकः ।। १० ।।

param evākṣaraṁ pratipadyate, sa yo ha vai tad acchāyam aśarīram alohitam śubhram akṣaraṁ vedayate; yas tu somya, sa sarvajñaḥ sarvo bhavati, tad eṣa ślokaḥ ।। 10 ।।

One who knows That as the shadowless, the bodiless, the colourless, the pure, the imperishable, he attains the Transcendental Imperishable, O Dear. He is the knower of everything; he is everything. As to this there is this verse:

Guru: Here we touch the crux of what this Upaniṣad teaches.

Seeker: In what sense?

G: The two preceding stanzas showed the Self as the source of both *prakṛti* and *puruṣa* aspects of existence; here it shows directly the nature and content of the Self, the final goal of all Vedāntic enquiry.

S: Why is *ātmā* considered *param* (the transcendental)?

G: Everything conceivable can be categorized either as *prakṛti* or *puruṣa*. *Ātmā*, the source of both as well as the abode of both, transcends both.

S: The Self is without attributes, according to Advaita Vedānta. Here we see the Self as having a number of attributes.

G: Though the Self seems to have attributes, It is not to be understood as the substance qualified by these attributes, and to that extent what appear to be attributes are not attributes at all. *Param* means that which is beyond everything that has attributes. Above all, every seeming attribute named here is really the negation of some other attribute.

S: The word *akṣara*, apart from denoting the imperishable, is also any letter of an alphabet. Is it significant in this context?

G: Yes, in the sense that it suggests the mono-syllable *AUṀ*, pronounced *OṀ*, the linguistic sign for the Imperishable Reality. Customarily treated as signifying God, *AUṀ* is worshipped by some as a deity, some repeat pronouncing it a certain number of times, often 108 as a spiritual practice.

S: Why is *AUṀ* treated as signifying God or *ātmā*?

G: The whole of the *Māṇḍūkya Upaniṣad* is an attempt to elaborate on the mono-syllable *AUṀ*. Better you read it along with the traditional commentaries of Gauḍapāda and Śaṅkara and some modern commentaries.

S: I shall read those books. Why is the Self considered bodiless (*aśarīra*)? Why can't we take the entire world, *prakṛti* and *puruṣa* together, as its body?

G: It is only a matter of difference in the points of view. To take the gold-ornament analogy, gold as the substance, though conceivable, is perceivable only in some form like that of an ornament. The imperishable gold never exists without some perishable form. Advaita Vedānta considers the causal substance alone as real and the apparent forms as mere illusory appearances, not having any existence of their own. This perspective is known as *sat-kāraṇa-vāda*, the theory that cause is the reality, which was preferred by Śaṅkara. Rāmānuja, the proponent of the Viśiṣṭādvaita school of Vedānta, on the other hand, considered both the substance and the apparent forms as real. His stand is known as *sat-kārya-vāda*, the theory that effect also is real.

S: Which one is acceptable to us?

G: As a method of approach the former is to be preferred. Yet both are different approaches to one reality. This difference in the ways of approach does in no way affect the nature and content of the reality searched for. How many points of view could there be concerning a single reality?

S: They could be as many as we fancy.

G: Are we here interested in the points of view or in the reality as such?

S: Only in the reality. But how can we approach it other than through some point of view?

G: This problem crops up when we go around the reality and assess it from outside.

S: Is there any way of saving us from this problem?

G: Yes, there is. Instead of perceiving the real from outside, one has to find oneness with the real, as an ornament feels oneness with gold, where the apparent form and substance, effect and cause, *kārya* and *kāraṇa*, are directly experienced as inseparable and non-dual. This realisation, in classical Vedānta, is known as *aparokṣānubhūti* or *aparokṣa-jñāna* (non-mediate experience or wisdom), and is denoted by the word *pratipadyate* (is attained) in the text. Attaining it, one does not see one's apparent form as different from the real, and therefore having a body is of no significance, in which sense, it is also our experience of bodilessness.

S: How is this theory named?

G: This is no theory at all. Reality is not to be established or proved theoretically; it is simply to be directly realised as one's own being.

S: Is colourlessness (*alohitam*) also to be understood likewise?

G: The word *alohitam* is interpretable both ways, as attributeless as also surcharged with attributes.

S: How is it so?

G: *Lohitam* means red in colour; *alohitam* is its opposite. Redness signifies *rajo-guṇa*, the active modality of nature, and thus stands for activity. *Alohitam* thus symbolises the actionlessness of the Self. It could also be interpreted as denial of grossness.

S: How?

G: Earth, the grossest of the five physical elements is considered red in colour. Denial of redness thus symbolises the denial of grossness. Redness also signifies richness and beauty, its absence stands also for the denial of all visual beauty and enjoyable richness. The next epithet *śubhram* (the pure) also adds to this implicit meaning.

Alohitam in an assertive sense means red lotus. I don't have to name its enjoyable positive qualities. The overwhelming positive qualities inherent in visualising the Supreme Self are not an attainment where attainer and attained are different; it is the attainment in which the attainer is lost in the attained, often compared to the state of a salt-doll that went to measure the depth of the sea. The word *pratipadyate* connotes such a merger.

S: Both the senses are so cogent that neither can be set aside.

G: Neither is intended to be set aside.

S: Then?

G: The word *alohitam* remains unaffected despite the two opposite interpretations. Likewise, the non-dual Reality remains unaffected despite viewing it from different points and being given different perspectives. Seen from the *sat* point of view it is one alone, attributeless; looked at from the *bhāva* point of view the apparent forms are many, each surcharged with many attributes. These opposing perspectives in no way affects the inseparable oneness of *sat* and *bhāva*, comparable to the unseparability of gold and ornaments. This neutrality is also suggested by the word *śubhram* (the pure).

G: It is said, "One who knows That, is the knower of everything." What does it mean?

G: An ornament, on knowing the gold-reality in itself, is knowing not merely the gold in it alone, but the gold-reality in all the ornaments. Forgoing its own particular form, it identifies itself with all ornaments, it sees itself in all ornaments. So too, one who realises the reality in himself as the all-pervading *ātmā* forgoes his individual being and finds oneness with the whole. He becomes the knower of everything, he becomes everything. The *Īśa Upaniṣad* puts this final attainment of Vedāntic search thus: He sees everything in himself and himself in everything. He finds nothing to be despised. When touching the core of the teaching in this fashion, no Upaniṣad claims it as its own discovery or contribution. Instead, the *ṛṣi* says that this secret had been known to *ṛṣi*s of the past; the *Praśna Upaniṣad* also is no exception. The present chapter concludes with the next stanza quoting a verse from another *ṛṣi*.

> विज्ञानात्मा सह देवैश्च सर्वैः
> प्राणा भूतानि संप्रतिष्ठन्ति यत्र।
> तदक्षरं वेदयते यस्तु सोम्य
> स सर्वज्ञः सर्वमेवाविवेशेति ॥ ११ ॥
>
> *vijñānātmā saha devaiś ca sarvaiḥ*
> *prāṇā bhūtāni saṁpratiṣṭhanti yatra* ।
> *tad akṣaraṁ vedayate yas tu somya*
> *sa sarvajñaḥ sarvam evāviveśa iti* ॥ 11 ॥

Aware of the Imperishable in which dwell the knowing self (*vijñānātmā*), *prāṇa*s and all beings along with all gods, one becomes, O Dear, the omniscient pervading everything.

Seeker: The idea in this quoted verse is much like the crux of the teaching seen in the previous stanza. One new concept appearing in this verse is that of *vijñānātmā*. What is it?

Guru: Pure Consciousness in essence, the Self is never known to us as such. Our experience is only of specific knowledge, of the many forms it assumes unceasingly. The mind that knows in each such situation is a form assumed by Pure Consciousness. The knowledge possessed by mind, and the objects thus known are also nothing but the same Consciousness appearing in those forms. All these factors involved in every situation of knowing are inclusively signified by *vijñānātmā*.

S: The word *vijñāna*, in Vedānta, sometimes stands for its final goal, *mokṣa*, the final liberation. Is it in any way implicit here?

G: That sense is also admissible when seen from the discipline point of view. The function of Consciousness in general was our concern so far. A seeker's well disciplined enquiry for Reality is also a function of Consciousness and is known as *sādhanā*. The result aimed at, then is called *sādhya* which is but *mokṣa* (final liberation) itself. In this particular sense *mokṣa* is the *vijñāna* aspect of Vedāntic wisdom or *jñāna*.

S: There is a reference to gods here along with the *vijñānātmā*. What does it indicate?

G: The meaning of gods we have discussed in detail before. Gods, in the Vedic context, are the imaginary inhabitants of the imaginary heaven. Earth, heaven and hell or any other imaginable worlds can exist only within the transcendental Self, as apparent manifest forms of the Self. Related to our individual being, the gods are our sense-organs.

S: Is the usage *bhūtāni* (beings) of any special significance?

G: Do you remember where we began our enquiry in this Upaniṣad?

S: Yes, by trying to find out how all beings were born.

G: The beings were called *prajas* then; here they are called *bhūta*s, meaning those which have come into being or emerged. We are thus touching our starting point as reaching the finishing point.

Fifth Question

पञ्चमः प्रश्नः

अथ हैनं शैब्यः सत्यकामः पप्रच्छ — स यो ह वै तद्भगवन् मनुष्येषु प्रायणान्तमोङ्कारमभिध्यायीत, कतमं वाव स तेन लोकं जयतीति। तस्मै स होवाच ॥ १ ॥

atha hainaṁ śaibyaḥ satyakāmaḥ papraccha—sa yo ha vai tad bhagavan manuṣyeṣu prāyaṇāntam oṁkāram abhidhyāyīta, katamaṁ vāva sa tena lokaṁ jayatīti । tasmai sa hovāca ॥ 1 ॥

Then Satyakāma, son of Śibi, asked him (Pippalāda): Venerable Sir, which of the many worlds does he among men conquer by meditating on *AUṀ* till death? To him Pippalāda said:

Seeker: This question doesn't look sequential to the assertion made at the end of the previous chapter.

Guru: The last chapter ended with bringing out the finality of Vedāntic teaching, stating its ultimate benefit as well. The attainment of this goal requires a well defined means. This means, meditating on *AUṀ*, is the topic discussed in this chapter. Any such disciplined effort to attainment is called *sādhanā*; the attainment of the goal is *siddhi* and the one who attains, *sādhaka*.

S: Why is this particular means chosen here?

G: *AUṀ*, you know, is the verbal sign for God or *Brahman*, and so meditating on *AUṀ* is the best means of attaining *Brahman*.

S: How does *AUṀ* signify *Brahman*?

G: Anything known is communicable through language using words. Each word has a meaning that can be experienced objectively or subjectively. The sum total of all such experiences constitutes the visible world (*dṛśya-prapañca*) for each of us. Each experience is represented by a word and the aggregate of such words constitutes the world of words (*śabda-prapañca*). All the words are inter-related the way all experienced worldly entities are inter-related.

Even as every entity in the visible world has a corresponding word representing it, *Brahman*, the Reality underlying all visible entities, also needs a word to represent it. While the words representing visible, perishable entities are pershable (*kṣara*), the word representing the Imperishable has also necessarily to be imperishable (*akṣara*). *AUṀ* is therefore considered *ekākṣara*, meaning the one Imperishable as well as the mono-syllable. *A, U* and *Ṁ* are the first, middle and last vowels of the Sanskrit alphabet. Vowels being that which animates consonants in creating words of all languages, *AUṀ* is the condensation of the vital force of Sanskrit alphabet, and therefore taken to represent the living force behind the world of words, the sign of *Brahman*. More details of it you may have got from the *Māṇḍūkya Upaniṣad*.

S: Muttering *AUṀ* a certain number of times, sometimes along with counting beads, is a spiritual practice for some. Is it the meditation understood here?

G: Not exactly, yet it is not excluded. *AUṀ* is a word. Uttering of every word results in the bursting out of a meaning in our mind; *AUṀ* is the word which, when uttered, results in the bursting out in our mind of the meaning of the all-inclusive Reality, which is ungraspable.

S: What do you mean?

G: I shall elaborate on it. Arun is our friend. As I utter the name the idea of that particular person bursts out in your mind, a psychological factor, known as *sphoṭa* in India. If I say only 'our friends', the idea bursting forth in your mind will be something general and indistinct. On my saying 'human beings' the idea formulated is even more general and indistinct. The ultimate limit upto which this generalisation can be taken to, excludes nothing. There has to be a word that makes this all-inclusive Reality its meaning. That word is *AUṀ*. The meaning that bursts out on its uttering is the most ungraspable, yet an awareness of the whole, an experience of effulgence where even the distinctness of the experiencer, the experienced and the experience gets effaced. It is the world attained by meditating (*abhidhyāna*) *AUṀ*.

S: Are there many worlds to be conquered thus?

G: Yes there are. The word *lokam*, literally meaning that which can be looked at, stands for the world. What is seen when looked at depends upon how one looks at it, which in turn depends upon the knowledge one has gained, one's attitudes and value notions, and many such factors, and therefore, though the world we *look at* is the same, what each of us *actually sees* is different. The same is true with meditating on *AUṀ*; what is visualised in meditation depends on how its meaning is conceived. The coming verses, for this reason, cite three ways of *AUṀ*-meditation and the three different worlds thus attained.

S: Satyakāma's question implies the seeker meditating *AUṀ* till death, but we know *AUṀ* stands for the Immortal. Does it mean that the meditator will reach a particular world after death if he meditates *AUṀ* till death?

G: The word *prāyaṇāntam*, translated here as 'till death', literally means 'until the termination of the forward journey'. This forward journey is all the transactions a person goes through. The awareness that the one and only birthless and deathless Reality endures in and through all such countless worldly transactions, gives the personal life and its transactions a new character and dimension. Leading one's own personal life with such an attitude is to be called *prāyaṇa*. That personal appearance and its transactions terminate at a point of time called death, but the Reality underlying them has to continue. *Antam* meaning end, *prāyaṇāntam* means, the termination of the apparent transactions of an apparent being. What we usually understand by death is the annihilation of an existing being, while *prāyanāntam* implies the continuance of what is real while the apparent form terminates.

एतद् वै सत्यकाम परं चापरं च ब्रह्म यदोङ्कारः।
तस्माद् विद्वानेतेनैवायतनेनैकतरमन्वेति ।। २ ।।

etad vai satyakāma paraṁ ca aparaṁ ca brahma yad oṁkāraḥ ।
tasmād vidvān etenaivāyatanenaikataram anveti ॥ 2 ॥

That which is (meant by) the sound *AUṀ*, O Satyakāma, is verily the transcendental and immanent *Brahman*. With it alone, therefore, for means, the wise one pursues and attains either of the two.

Seeker: *AUṀ* is first equated to transcendental and immanent *Brahman*; then it says those who meditate on *AUṀ* attain either of the two. In effect thus it seems to say, only those who meditate on *AUṀ* attain *AUṀ*.

Guru: Yes, that is the simplest way to put the vision intended to be conveyed. As nothing is excluded from the ambit of *AUṀ*, attaining anything is attaining *AUṀ*; attaining *AUṀ* is attaining anything. The wise seeker (*vidvān*) or *sādhaka*, the search (*sādhanā*) and the goal attained (*siddhi*) are all therefore to be inclusively visualised within *AUṀ*, as forming its details.

S: How to differentiate *para-brahman* and *apara-brahman*?

G: *Brahman*, as the imperishable, eternal, invisible, inconceivable, abstract substance underlying all the apparent forms of the world, as gold in ornaments, is conceived as *para-brahman*; and *Brahman* as apprearing in all the perishable, transient, visible, conceivable, concrete forms of the world, as ornament-appearances of gold, is to be understood as *apara-brahman*. Yet, though conceived distinctly as two, neither exists without the other.

S: Why are the two named as if distinct, creating all these speculative problems?

G: *Brahma-vidyā*, what the Upaniṣads teach, is a *śāstra* or science. *Śāstra* means that which gives certitude, here the certitude sought is about *Brhaman* or *ātmā*. Why do we need such a search?

S : Because we are inquisitive about the reality underlying everything, the cause of our own origin and being.

G: Appearances are many, our search is for the one reality underlying all. Do you think, even on knowing the one reality, the multiplicity of forms will cease to appear?

S: Not at all.

G: We need then a method of arriving at certitude where the apparent many and the real one meet non-dually, where neither of the two nullifies the other, where reference to the two is inevitable. Such a reference to the two — *para-brahman* and *apara-brahman* — does not mean they exist separately or that they are separable. Their separateness merely in our concept and is to be abolished conceptually so that their oneness remains unaffected. The reference to the dual aspects of *para-brahman* and *apara-brahman* is therefore significant methodologically, only as a means for attaining the non-dual *Brahman*. Once the non-dual goal is attained, the two are to be given up, often compared to pricking out one thorn with another and finally giving up both. Considering their distinctness as of ontological significance causes confusion at least in the minds of novices; they start thinking of two *brahmans* existing in different realms, as it were, in complete violation of the basic tenets of all Vedāntic teaching.

S: Who is the *vidvān*, the learned seeker?

G: He is the one who sees unity and multiplicity unitively, one who is familiar with the precise methodology of transcending all dualities.

S: What does he take to as means, *AUṀ* or *Brahman*? Here it says, "with it alone as means, the wise one attains either of the two".

G: As a spiritual practice it is meditating *AUṀ*, but, *AUṀ* meaning *Brahman*, meditating *AUṀ* means meditating *Brahman*. The original word *āyatanam*, translated here as 'means' literally means 'one's own home'. Everyone's proper and unfailing home is *Brahman*, the Reality in onself; no one lives away from it. Even my meditating on *AUṀ*, is a minute element of the creative self-expression of *Brahman*, therefore not outside *Brahman*. With *Brahman* itself thus functioning as the means of attaining *Brahman*, equating *Brahman* and *AUṀ* becomes all the more meaningful.

S: Who pursues whom and attains whom?

G: The original word is *anveti* (*anu* + *eti*), *eti* meaning 'attains' and the prefix *anu*, 'by pursuing or following'. In the simplest sense, the wise one, by pursuing the meditation, attains *Brahman*. But it is not a pursuit similar to tracking a person. Given that every event in this world is creative self-expression of *Brahman*, every event, our own meditating *AUṀ* not excluded, pursues *Brahman*; we as seekers are pursuing *Brahman*. The question of who pursues whom is thus irrelevant; *Brahman* alone is, It pursues Itself. 'Attaining either of the two' does not indicate the possibility of two alternative goals. The wise one can meditate on *AUṀ* or *Brahman* as the abstract Substance that underlies everything. He then forgoes his identification with phenomenal appearance and finds himself one with *Brahman*. He can also meditate on *AUṀ* or *Brahman* as having this world for its apparent form; then he sees himself as having no existence apart from the total world. Both are attainments of the wise; what is attained is one final goal. How one directs one's meditation depends on one's personal choice, which in turn depends on one's personal traits. No general rule is to be followed here. Strictly speaking, each person has to have his own way of meditating.

स यद्येकमात्रमभिध्यायीत स तेनैव संवेदितस्तूर्णमेव जगत्यामभिसंपद्यते। तमृचो मनुष्यलोकमुपनयन्ते, स तत्र तपसा ब्रह्मचर्येण श्रद्धया संपन्नो महिमानमनुभवति ॥ ३ ॥

sa yady eka-mātram abhidhyāyīta, sa tenaiva saṁveditas tūrṇam eva jagatyām abhisaṁpadyate । *tam ṛco manuṣya-lokam upanayante, sa tatra tapasā brahmacaryeṇa śraddhayā saṁpanno mahimānam anubhavati* ॥ 3 ॥

Meditating one sound unit (*A*), one, enlightened accordingly, no sooner attains this world of changefulness (*jagat*). The *Ṛgveda* verses lead him unto the human world. Endowed with *tapas*, *brahmacarya* and *śraddhā*, there he enjoys greatness.

Seeker: What is *mātrā*?

Guru: A technical term in Sanskrit prosody, *mātrā* is a unit of sound measured by uttering an unstressed syllable. *AUṀ* is uttered in four such units, each represented by the three letters and the silence that follows. What those three letters and the silence stand for you must have learnt from the *Māṇḍūkya Upaniṣad*. Both appended to the *Atharvaveda*, the *Praśna Upaniṣad* presupposes familiarity with the *Māṇḍūkya Upaniṣad*; more so as the latter is more basic and ancient.

S: How does one who meditate on the first *mātrā* of *AUṀ* attain this changeful world?

G: Any attainment is in accordance with what one is interested in. *A*, the first *mātrā* of *AUṀ*, represents the world experienced in the waking state; one who mediates on that world as of the highest value, attains all that is attainable in that world. Attainment of a higher world by one who thinks only of the changeful worldly values is quite unimaginable.

S: How do the *Ṛgveda* verses lead such a person to the human world?

G: Man, the being in whom biological evolution has supposedly reached the highest complexity, is still subject to all transformations and vagaries of nature. What really makes him superior to other beings is his possessing knowledge as well as knowing himself as possessing knowledge. Vedas, in principle, are the embodiments of the sum total of all knowledge man can ever have. Of the four Vedas the *Ṛgveda* is the most ancient, the most important, the most interested in worldly matters and pleasures, the most tempting. The man who meditates on *AUṀ* with the realm *A* alone, the realm of worldly experiences alone, in his purview, attains the benefits attainable in that world, represented here by the *Ṛgveda*. Yet it need not necessarily be an indulgence in worldly pleasures for ever. Having that knowledge might perchance induce him to search for higher realities and higher values — another possibility in the human world. An inquisitive mind, willingness to undertake the search in spite of various obstacles and difficulties, one-pointed attention in the one Reality, and full faith in the possiblity of realising it, are all natural there. All this is indicated by the words *tapas*, *brahmacarya* and *śraddhā*. Such a possibility also could be seen held high in the *Ṛgveda*.

S: Now I recollect: Pippalāda asked the six seekers to stay with him an year with the same *tapas*, *brahmacarya* and *śraddhā*.

G: It shows how thought develops in this Upaniṣad with consistencey, along a well conceived line.

अथ यदि द्विमात्रेण मनसि सम्पद्यते सोऽन्तरिक्षं यजुर्भिरुन्नीयते सोमलोकम्।
स सोमलोके विभूतिमनुभूय पुनरावर्तते ॥ ४ ॥

atha yadi dvi-mātreṇa manasi sampadyate । *so'ntarikṣam*
yajurbhir unnīyate somalokam । *sa somaloke vibhūtim*
anubhūya punar āvartate ॥ 4 ॥

Meditating the two sound units (of *AUṀ*), one attains mind (*manas*). The formulas of the *Yajurveda* lead him up to *soma-loka*, the mid-world. Having experienced prosperity there, he returns.

Seeker: The first two *mātrās* together or the second *mātrā* alone, which one is to be meditated on, according to this verse?

Guru: A understanding of the first *mātrā A* and its meaning being a prerequisite for understanding the second one *U*, it should be the two together that is meditated on.

S: How does this meditation concur with the meaning of *U* according to the *Māṇḍūkya Upanaiṣad*?

G: The letter *U* is the linguistic sign for the dream experiences. The consciousness in that state, known as *taijasa*, knows and enjoys objects of its own creation. Otherwise it is just like the waking state represented by *A*.

S: What we see as real in the waking state turns out to be unreal in the dreaming state; what we see as real in the dreaming state becomes unreal in the waking state. To decide which is real and which is unreal is quite impossible.

G: That shows the conditional nature of the realness of these two experiences. Neither is absolutely real. What is absolutely and undoubtedly real in both is Consciousness alone. How all such experiences form part of a lengthy dream, mind creating everything to be enjoyed by itself, where mind is the essence of everything, we have already examined in detail. The Upaniṣad therefore asserts, the one who meditates on the two *mātrās A* and *U* of *AUṀ* reaches mind.

S: Why is the world reached by him called *soma-loka*?

G: *Soma* is the moon, the symbol of cosmic mind in the mythological language of India. The individual mind, while dreaming, creates a world and enjoys it. The cosmic mind in the same way creates the entire world from itself and enjoys it. To be led upwards to the world of moon therefore allegorically represents the meditator becoming sublimated to the realm of this all-inclusive mind.

S: How is the *Yajurveda* instrumental in this self-sublimating process?

G: The *Yajurveda* is a collection of some Ṛgvedic verses modified for the purpose of *yajña*s aimed at attaining certain favourable results. It is mind that conceives of such rituals and fancies the achievement of desired results. I hope you know how this concept of *yajña* originated.

S: Yes. We have discussed it in detail at the beginning. It symbolises offering back to nature what was wrongly considered as ours.

G: Unaware of that philosophy and psychology of *yajña*, our mind, enchanted by the prospect of having more and more pleasures, misinterprets the very *yajña* principle and misuses it as a means of ensuring more pleasures. Such was the origin of the *Yajurveda* and its rituals, all a mental manipulation of pleasure-seeking man. Only those who become aware of how our mind manipulates things and pulls us down to the world of pleasures and resultant sufferings, get induced to save themselves. The very *Yajurveda* contains teachings on how to save us from such sorry states and to lead us to the *soma-loka*.

S: What is the *vibhūti* experienced by such a person in the *soma-loka*, the moon-world?

G: The state in which enjoyables are in plenty, the very state coveted by ritualists, is called *vibhūti* in the worldly sense. But philosophically it means the specific form in which something has come into being. Everything, as a dream, we know, comes into being from one mind, to be enjoyed by itself, and therefore is a *vibhūti* of mind.

S: What is meant by 'he returns'?

G: One cannot go on dreaming for ever; waking is essential, to go back to dreaming again. The cosmic dream of the cosmic mind also repeats itself altering its moods and patterns, and for that reason no one is aware that what we go on seeing here is merely a dream. The continuance of this dream is not like the non-stop rotating of a fly wheel; it is more like the rolling on of a chariot wheel. Every new repetition encounters a new terrain, making every moment of life a novel one. It is a repeated creative self-expression of mind.

S: First I thought, meditating on *A*, *AU* and *AUṀ* are stages of an ascending order; now it seems there is no such order. On the contrary, meditating on *A* seems inferior to meditating on *AU*, the former had in it at least the prospect of attaining greatness, the latter does not give even such a hope.

G: To think of such an ascending order shows the conditioning of our mind. Interpolating such notions into the vision of a *ṛṣi* is not just. What would be proper is to search for the structural vision the *ṛṣi* originally had in his mind.

S: No such an order is evident here.

G: The order of the states of consciousness, you remember, was changed by the *ṛṣi* to *suṣupti-jāgrat-svapna*, instead of the usual order *jāgrat-svapna-suṣupti*. It shows the *ṛṣi* had an ordering of his own in his mind.

The three letters symbolise the three states of consciousness; these states and their experiences constitute the world. The world we know has a structural coherence of its own; the knowledge of the world — the experiences at the three states — should also be of the same structure if it is true knowledge; what the three letters sysmbolise is this knowledge necessarily symbolising the same structure too. This common structural perfection of the world, the knowledge of the world and its sysmbols has been rendered easy to understand, by Nataraja Guru by representing it graphically.

The waking and the dreaming states are both of transactional status and value, one gross and the other subtle, one exterior and the other interior. The horizontal axis of the graph stands for this world, the positive pole (+) representing the waking state and negative pole (–) the dreaming state. The habit of our transactional mind is to move in between these two poles horizontally. Tho two poles symbolise the human world and the world of the moon. Behind both is the causal Consciousness. Nothing is known of it, it is conceived of as being in deep-sleep; pure effulgence in essence, it is represented as the *sūrya-loka*, the world of the sun, to be dwelt on in the next stanza. The substance underlying both the transactional states is attributeless and is symbolised by the negative pole of the vertical axis. Though *cit* (consciousness) in essence, what is predominant in this state is its *sat* (existence) aspect. This *sat-cit*, overwhelming with its own inherent creative urge for self-expression, rises to the domain of the transactional world assuming the forms of both subject and object in both waking dreaming states. One who is aware of his own transactional existence and awareness as arising from *sat-cit*, as its self-unfoldment, experiences the Happiness (*ānanda*) described in the next stanza.

Nothing that matters in a systematic enquiry of a seeker — the actualities of life, the one underlying Reality, the final goal of life — is excluded from this scheme of correlation (see Figure).

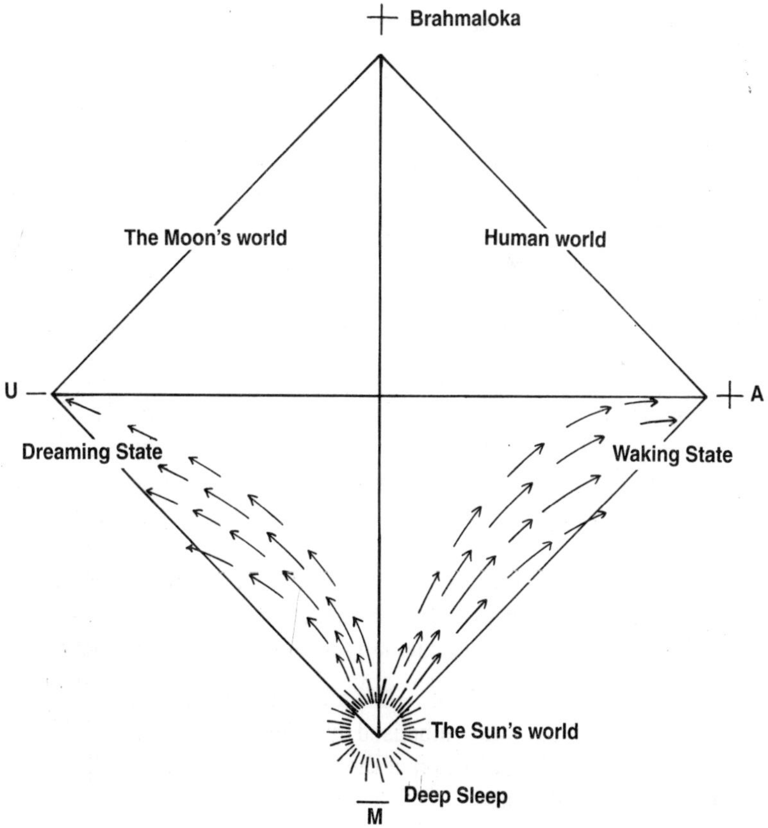

S: Why can't we treat this scheme, itself as interpolated by Nataraja Guru into this context unwarrantedly.

G: It is not a scheme of correlation-newly invented by Nataraja Guru; he was only bringing to light something already hiding in all the scriptures of the world. Like a master-key, it helps open many a mystery hidden in the scriptures, and to that extent it could be considered an original contribution of Nataraja Guru to philosophy, the more so to scriptural philsosophy.

यः पुनरेतं त्रिमात्रेणौमित्येतेनैवाक्षरेण परं पुरुषमभिध्यायीत स तेजसि सूर्ये संपन्नः। यथा पादोदरस्त्वचा विनिर्मुच्यत एवं ह वै स पाप्मना विनिर्मुक्तः स सामभिरुन्नीयते ब्रह्मलोकं स एतस्माज्जीवघनात्परात्परं पुरिशयं पुरुषमीक्षते, तदेतौ श्लोकौ भवतः ॥ ५ ॥

yaḥ punar etaṁ tri-mātreṇa om ity etenaivākṣareṇa paraṁ puruṣam abhidhyāyīta sa tejasi sūrye saṁpannaḥ ।
yathā pādodaras tvacā vinirmucyata evaṁ ha vai sa pāpmanā vinirmuktaḥ sa sāmabhir unnīyate brahma-lokaṁ sa etasmāj jīvaghanāt parāt-paraṁ puriśayaṁ puruṣam īkṣate, tad etau ślokau bhavataḥ ॥ 5 ॥

Meditating on the highest *puruṣa* as the syllable *AUṀ* with its three *mātrās*, one finds himself in the Sun, the world of effulgence. Even as snakes get rid of their slough, so too he becomes free of sin. He is led by the *Sāma* chants to the world of *Brahman*. He, as a living entity, sees the higher than the highest *puruṣa*, the dweller in the city. As to this there are these two verses:

Seeker: The two preceding stanzas did not make any mention of meditating on *AUṀ*, but only of the one *mātrā* (*A*) and two *mātrās* (*AU*). Meditating on *AUṀ* is mentioned only in this stanza. Why is it so?

Guru: *AUṀ* becomes *AUṀ* only when all the three *mātrās* are treated together as one. What was symbolised by *A* and *AU* were not *AUṀ*, but merely the limited field of vision of the one who meditated on them as representing the ultimate.

S: Why is *puruṣa* qualified as the higher than the highest (*parāt param*)? Is it in any way related to the *para* and *apara* distinction of *Brahman* made at the beginning of this chapter?

G: Yes, the two contexts are closely related. The *parāt-param* this stanza signifies is beyond the distinction of *parā* and *aparā*. Meditating on this reference, along with the significance of the third *mātrā* described in the *Māṇḍūkya Upaniṣad*, may be more enlightening.

S: How is the third *mātrā* conceived in the *Māṇḍūkya Upaniṣad?*

G: The *mātrā* represented by the letter *Ṁ* stands for the unconscious happiness experienced in deep-sleep (*suṣupti*), the state in which no desire arises, and no dream is dreamt. No question of a multiplicity in experience arises in such a state. All multiplicities, the *Māṇḍūkya Upaniṣad* says, merge in the unconscious unity of *suṣupti*.

S: Do they merge with the darkness of *suṣupti*?

G: The seed-like consciousness in that state, though non-functional is not darkness in content; it is pure consciousness in essence, called *prajñāna-ghana* by the Upaniṣad.

S: What is *prajñāna-ghana*?

G: Literally, of the content of consciousness. As an experience, it is the state of the self's experiencing its own *ānanda*-content, yet remaining unconscious of it.

S: Never having been conscious of, how could such a state be considered as existing?

G: The only evidence of its existing is our feeling, after sound sleep, "I had a sound sleep." The soundness, experienced while asleep, was not known in that state. Only on waking up is it recalled. A mystery indeed, on becoming aware of it, one realises that the consciousness which unconsciously experiences the happiness of deep-sleep is nothing but God (*Īśvara*). The *Māṇḍūkya Upaniṣad* therefore depicts it as the Lord of All, the All-Knowing, the indweller in everything, the prime source of all, and into which all merge at dissolution.

S: How does the *suṣupti* experience differ from *turīya*?

G: The state of *turīya*, literally 'the fourth', signified by the silence that follows *AUṀ*, is also elucidated in the *Māṇḍūkya Upaniṣad*; but the entire description is a negative one, saying what it is not. It says:

> It is neither inwardly known nor outwardly known nor known both ways together; it is not even the essence of consciousness; it is neither known nor unknown; it is imperceptible, ineffable, incomprehensible, undefinable, unthinkable. It is the essence of the awareness of the one Self wherein the entire world merges back. It is peacefulness (*śāntam*), pure goodness (*śivam*). It is non-dual.

But Narayana Guru, a sage of modern times, gives a more positive definition in terms of mystical experience, in his *Ātmopadeśa-Śatakam*, thus:

> *Turīya* awareness is knowing from top to bottom what is bottomless and topless. — Verse 28

What differentiates *turīya* from *suṣupti* is this: Consciously experiencing the inner content of the beginningless and endless Self from beginning to end is *turīya*. To have the same experience unconsciously is *suṣupti*. The introductory textbooks of Vedānta therefore consider *suṣupti* as a state in which the Self is shrouded by the veil of ignorace (*avidyā*); in *turīya* this shroud is absent.

S: This Upaniṣad does not make any reference to *turīya*. Why is it so?

G: *Turīya*, even according to the *Māṇḍūkya Upaniṣad* is an ineffable experience; the linguistic symbol, if any that can represent it, is only the silence that follows the uttering of the three *mātrā*s of *AUṀ*. The *Māṇḍūkya Upaniṣad* therefore says it is *amātra* (*mātrā*-less). The *Praśna Upaniṣad* prefers to maintain silence — a silence with ample implicit suggestiveness. The *Brahma-loka* (the world of *Brahman*) to which the meditator is led, is none other than the *turīya* experience.

The causal consciousness, as *sat*, was shown at the vertical minus of the graphic representation. The same *sat*, as *cit* (consciousness), uninfluenced by either of the sides, ascends and attains a state of becoming aware of its own *ānanda* content. This realisation of *saccidānanda*, referred to as the attaining of *Brahma-loka*, in essence is the *turīya* experience.

S: How does one of such an attainment of wisdom free himself of all sins? Does it mean that it expiates him of all his sins?

G: No. A subtle dialectical secret is implicit here.

S: What is it?

G: How do you relate the two: 'to be free of all sins' and 'to attain *Brahma-loka*'?

S: As the former leading to the latter.

G: No. To be free of sins itself means 'attaining *Brahma-loka*'. The event is one; looked at from the point of view of actions it is to become free of sins, looked at from the point of view of wisdom it is the attainment of *Brahman*. The two statements are simply like the two sides of a coin; what is real is only the coin, but it needs reference to the two sides to be able to recognise it. Attaining *Brahman*, one finds oneself free of the sense of sin and merit, thus free of all sins; this sense of freedom is what makes the attainment of *Brahma-loka* of value for the seeker, who lives in this world, suggested by the words 'as a living entity'. This is one of the instances of *ṛṣi*s adopting the dialectical method or *yogic* way of expression to express verbally something that is essentially ineffable.

S: What is really meant by sin (*pāpa*)?

G: A religious term, it means doing anything forbidden in the scriptures, and not doing what is enjoined in them.

S: Not concerned with any such action or ritual, this context does not give room for such a concept of sin.

G: The wisdom context has its own concept of sin.

S: What is it?

G: The world as a whole is in a state of eternal flux, and it follows a structural system of its own, though incomprehensible to the human mind. Our emergence and existence are also part of that flow. Such of our activities as are fully in agreement with that flow of nature are to be considered meritorious (*puṇya*). Those activities which do not agree with the flow of total nature, which do not have any consideration for the whole world and all other beings in it, which are guided by one's own personal gains, are sinful actions (*pāpa-karmas*).

S: How is it that the *Sāman* chants lead one to the world of *Brahman*?

G: The *Sāmaveda* is the musical rendering of some verses of the *Ṛgveda*, and therefore its verses are customarily called *Samagāḥ* (the *Sāman* chants). More experiential than thought provoking, they lead the chanters to high realms of inner joy, culminating in the ecstacy of realising *Brahman*.

S: What is the significance of the seeker, as a living entity, seeing the higher than the highest *puruṣa*?

G: We have just seen how we recognise a coin with its two sides as references. Once we know the real content of the coin, we realise also that all similar coins have the same content. We are all in the place of coins, having one inner content, the non-dual Self. Put conversely, we are concretised forms of one and the same Self-Reality. Each individual that arises thus and lives a while, is called a *jīva*, a living entity, a word usually misinterpreted as the Sanskrit equivalent to soul. Etymologically the word means, that which sustains through respiration (*jīva-prāṇane*). Each individual being (*jīva*) is thus a *pura* (city) wherein resides the non-dual Self. An individual, with this awareness, looking for the higher than highest *puruṣa*, sees Him as the indwelling content of each of these cities.

तिस्रो मात्रा मृत्युमत्यः प्रयुक्ता अन्योन्यसक्ता अनविप्रयुक्ताः।
क्रियासु बाह्याभ्यन्तरमध्यमासु सम्यक्प्रयुक्तासु न कम्पते ज्ञः ॥ ६ ॥

tisro mātrā mṛtyumatyaḥ prayuktā
anyonya-saktā anaviprayuktāḥ ।

kriyāsu bāhyābhyantara-madhyamāsu
samyak-prayuktāsu na kampate jñaḥ ॥ 6 ॥

The three *mātrās*, put to use separately, lead to death. Seen thus as mutually attached, each is not inapplicable separately in activities properly performed, whether within, without or midway between. But the one who knows thus does not waver.

Guru: Verses quoted from a former *ṛṣi*, this and the next, substantiate the principle of meditation elucidated above. How to meditate on the three *mātrās* properly, and the dangers of going wrong are also made clear.

Seeker: It says, the three *mātrās* used separately in meditation lead to death. Does it mean that those who meditate thus have to face death?

G: It may better be looked at from another point. The three *mātrās*, you know, are mere linguistic signs representing three states assumed by one and the same Consciousness. What is real as substance in those states is one Consciousness alone. Do you think we can get a comprehensive vision of this one Consciousness through meditating on any one of its states?

S: No.

G: Consciousness lives as Reality. A living person's amputated limb is never considered as the person; so too meditating on any limb of *AUṀ*, treating that limb as the whole, is meaningless, being a meditation on the dead limb of a living Reality. The three *mātrās* are therefore said to be subject to death if used separately in meditating.

It also means, one who meditates on any particular limb alone as real, faces death.

S: How?

G: The Reality symbolised by *AUṀ*, and meditated as *AUṀ*, we know, is birthless and deathless; the goal of the meditating seeker too is the attainment of immortality — the realisation of his oneness with the Immortal Reality. Is it possible for anyone, meditating on the dead aspects or dead limbs of Reality, to attain the living Immortal Reality?

S: Not at all.

G: Until and unless one realises his own self as the Immortal Reality, he finds himself in the ocean of birth and death. The one who meditates on any praticular limb, taking that limb alone as real and whole, for that reason, does not transcend the realm where birth and death seem real, and thus is subject to death.

S: Why can't all meditate on *AUṀ* as of the three *mātrās*?

G: Though such is the wish of the Upaniṣadic *ṛṣi*, it needs as prerequisite a clear understanding of the constituent limbs and what they represent?

S: Why?

G: In a living person we see also his distinct limbs, each having its own function. So too while meditating on *AUṀ* the seeker has to be aware of each of its limbs and their role in making the whole. Each *mātrā*, for this reason, it is said, is not to be used separately. Proper meditation, in other words, needs to visualise unity and multiplicity as pertaining to a non-dual whole. This subtle aspect is given emphasis to in the *Bhagavad Gītā* also when it says:

> Through wisdom sacrifice, others
> meditate on Me as unity and multiplicity,
> as facing everywhere in various ways. — IX.15

S: What are the exterior, interior and in-between activities?

G: Part of a quotation, these words are not of the *ṛṣi* of the *Praśna Upaniṣad*. Neither are we sure whether these words were uttered in relation to the same context of thinking. Yet, evidently there is a similarity between the *jāgrat-svapna-suṣupti* states and the exterior, mid-way and interior activities.

S: What is the 'properly performed activity'?

G: The Reality meditated on is not inert and inactive; it is creative and active; the one who meditates too is so. Creativity in him reaches its zenith when meditating on *AUṀ*. The 'properly performed activity' is thus both of the Reality meditated on, and of the meditating seeker. The merger of the creativity of the two in Self-realisation results in and ensures that he remains unwavering.

ऋग्भिरेतं यजुर्भिरन्तरिक्षं सामभिर्यत्तत्कवयो वेदयन्ते।
तामोङ्कारेणैवायतनेनान्वेति विद्वान् यत्तच्छान्तमजरममृतमभयं परं चेति ।। ७ ।।

ṛgbhir etaṁ, yajurbhir antarikṣaṁ,
sāmabhir yat tat kavayo vedayante ।

tam oṁkāreṇaivāyatanenānveti vidvān
yat tac chāntam ajaram amṛtam abhayaṁ paraṁ ceti ॥ 7 ॥

Through *Ṛg* verses (is attained) this world, through *Yajur* formulas the mid-region, through *Sāman* chants is attained that which the seers know. The wise one, with *AUṀ* alone as means, seeks and attains the tranquil, the unaging, the immortal, the fearless, the Supreme. Thus are the verses.

Seeker: This is also a quotation, and looks like a summarising of the whole chapter.

Guru: You are right, but it also answers the question asked by Satyakāma at the beginning of the chapter: that the one who meditates *AUṀ* transcends the realm of the three Vedas and attains *Brahman*.

S: Triple factors like the three worlds, the three Vedas, we have come across in this chapter — how could all of them be correlated?

G: To have a clear notion of how they are correlated is very important. All of them signify the tripartite nature of experiencing one Reality, *Brahman*, with various levels of understanding or related to different contexts of thinking. Together they could be tabulised as follows :

Ṛg Verses	*Yajur* Formulas	*Sāman* Chants
Human world	The Moon world	The world of *Brahman*
This world	Mid-world	The world of the seers
Waking state	Dreaming state	Deep-sleep
The gross	The subtle	The causal
Vaiśvānara	*Taijasa*	*Prājña*
First *mātrā*	Second *mātrā*	Third *mātrā*
A	*U*	*Ṁ*

All these together constitute the *aparā* (the immanent) *Brahman*, the *para Brahman* remaining conceivable.

Sixth Question

षष्ठः प्रश्नः

अथ हैनं सुकेशा भारद्वाजः पप्रच्छ। भगवन् हिरण्यनाभः कौसल्यो राजपुत्रो मामुपेत्यैतं प्रश्नमपृच्छत — षोडशकलं भारद्वाज पुरुषं वेत्थ? तमहं कुमारमब्रुवं नाहमिमं वेद यद्यहमिममवेदिषं कथं ते नावक्ष्यमिति। समूलो वा एष परिशुष्यति योऽनृतमभिवदति। तस्मान्नार्हाम्यनृतं वक्तुम्। स तूष्णीं रथमारुह्य प्रवव्राज। तं त्वा पृच्छामि क्वासौ पुरुष इति ॥ १ ॥

atha hainaṁ sukeśā bhāradvājaḥ papraccha । bhagavan hiraṇyanābhaḥ kausalyo rājaputro mām upetyaitaṁ praśnam apṛcchata — ṣoḍaśa-kalaṁ bhāradvāja puruṣaṁ vettha? tam ahaṁ kumāram abruvaṁ nāham imaṁ veda yady aham imam avediṣaṁ kathaṁ te nāvakṣyam iti । samūlo vā eṣa pariśuṣyati yo'nṛtam abhivadati । tasmān nārhāmy anṛtaṁ vaktuṁ । sa tūṣṇīṁ ratham āruhya pravavrāja । taṁ tvā pṛcchāmi kvāsau puruṣaḥ iti ॥ 1 ॥

Sukeśa, the son of Bharadvāja, then asked Pippalāda: Venerable Sir, Hiraṇyanābha, the son of the king of Kosala, approached me and asked, "Bhāradvāja, do you know the *puruṣa* of sixteen *kalās*?" I replied, "I know him not. If known to me why should I not tell you of him? Telling untruth, one verily becomes dried up right unto his root. I will not therefore tell you untruth." Mounting his chariot, he departed silent. Now I ask you of Him: Wherein is that *puruṣa*?

Seeker: The seekers who approached Pippalāda at the beginning were named in an order, the order was reversed when they started asking questions; each question was of a higher order than the preceding one. This final question of Sukeśa, on that account, should be of the highest order. Am I right?

Guru: Yes. This question is superior in two respects. First, concerning the *puruṣa* having sixteen *kalās*, the question, when answered, will reveal that the *puruṣa* and the sixteen *kalās* are inseparably one; the former stands for the unity of Reality and the latter for the multiplicity of appearances.

Secondly, the discussion in the Upaniṣad began with the problem, how all the beings originated; here the *puruṣa* is going to be shown as the creator of the sixteen *kalās*. Replacing creatures with *kalās*, the same question is answered here, as the Upaniṣad ends, in a subtler way leading to the finality of Vedāntic widsom. Having no existence apart from *puruṣa*, *kalās* are not really *born* of *puruṣa*. As a whole, our reaching the final certitude at the close of the Upaniṣad touches the very beginning, thus completing a full circle.

S: Sukeśa, instead of asking his own question, speaks of how he couldn't answer a question asked him by another, and repeats the same question to Pippalāda. Why he resorts to this indirect way?

G: The indirect way, Śaṅkara thinks, indicates its subtlety and rarity, as well as the strenuous effort required on the part of the seeker to find the final answer. Nevertheless, Sukeśa, it is evident, is not an ordinary seeker. In him, only this one question presumably remained unanswered. Hiraṇyanābha must have approached him taking him to be a *jñānin*.

S: May be Hiraṇyanāba's intention was to test Sukeśa's wisdom.

G: Sukeśa's words, "If known to me why should not I tell you of him", shows Hiraṇyanābha had no such intention. He himself might have attained Sukeśa's level of understanding; only such a person can ask a question like this. Sukeśa also perhaps had no idea as to what was the point to be cleared, to attain finality of wisdom. With certain seekers it so happens sometimes that they would feel that something remained to be cleared, but could not identify what it was. An incidental hint from someone else would be enough to help them get clear what they really wanted to know. For Sukeśa, Hiraṇyanābha's question was one such. Since then he must have been carrying this problem in his mind; here he has a chance to present it before Pippalāda.

S: Why did Hiraṇyanābha depart silent?

G: Finding that Sukeśa, who he thought capable of answering this final question, was of wisdom, only equal to his own, may have made Hiraṇyanābha silent.

S: *Hiraṇyanābha* being the son of a king, is emphasised here. Why is it so?

G: It is suggestive of the historical background of the Upaniṣads in general. The six seekers, stated as devoted to *Brahman* and intent on *Brahman*, are presumably brāhmaṇas by caste. Contexts of kṣatriyas (ruling class) teaching brāhmaṇas, and brāhmaṇas teaching kṣatriyas appear in the *Bṛhadāraṇyaka* and *Chāndogya Upaniṣads* as if there existed a sort of competition between the two classes over the issue of competence in teaching *Brahma-vidyā* which at times went even to the extent of kṣatriyas claiming that *Brahma-vidyā* had never dawned on brāhmaṇas. Jānśruti, a kṣatriya, was deridingly called śūdra (of the lowest caste) by Raikva, a brāhmaṇa. Historically kṣatriyas were leaders of the pre-Vedic original inhabitants of India and brāhmaṇas the priests of Vedic invaders. The Upaniṣads and their wisdom were an offshoot of the fusion of these two cultures, the leaders of both groups claiming superiority, echoed in references such as the present one. Hiraṇyanābha, kṣatriya, being the one who had identified the final question to be asked, stands one degree above Sukeśa.

S: Who is the *puruṣa* of sixteen *kalās*? Till now no *kalā* was seen associated with *puruṣa*?

G: The climax of the teaching having been arrived at in the fifth verse of the last chapter, where the Supreme (*param*) *puruṣa* was shown as attainable through meditating the three *mātrās* together of *AUṀ*, no other *puruṣa* remains to be known. It is the same *param purusa*, the dweller of the city, thus, that is conceived here as having sixteen *kalās*.

S: Where are these sixteen *kalās* from?

G: *Puruṣa* is the dweller of the city; any city must have various factors or limbs, which are abstracted and reduced to sixteen here. *Kalās* thus stand for the multiplicity of worldly appearances.

S: How was this number sixteen arrived at?

G: The original questioner is not Sukeśa but Hiraṇyanābha who already had this concept, possibly traditional, in his mind. What the *kalās* are, as Pippalāda conceives it, will become clear from the stanzas that follow; it will cover all factors from the subtler than the subtlest life principle (*prāṇa*) to the grosser than the grossest many worlds.

S: What does *kalā* really mean?

G: It is a word with a wide range of meanings: part of anything, the recognisable sign of anything, art, that portion of the moon which waxes or wanes in a single night, and so on. A tradition has it that *ka* means beginning and *la*, end, *kalā* thus means a minute part of something where the beginning itself is its end. The *kalā* concept plays a crucial role in the Śaiva school of Indian theology called Śaiva Siddhānta. That which is constituted of parts (*kalās*), the world, Śiva's body, is termed *sakala* by that school, and the partless Reality, Śiva himself, is qualified as *niṣkala* (the partless) or *kevala* (the abstract). *Māyā* makes *kalās* apparent in the otherwise unportioned Reality.

Traditional Indian poetic imagery maintains that full moon is constituted of sixteen *kalās*, named, Amṛta, Mānada, Pūṣa, Tuṣṭi, Puṣṭi, Rati, Dhṛti, Śaśinī, Candrikā, Kānti, Jyotsnā, Śrī, Prīti, Aṅgadā, Pūrṇā, Mṛtā. The most enchanting sight man ever sees, the moon signifies the Supreme Self contentment (*ānanda*) one experiences on Self-realisation, a *kalā* is its worldly expression; its waxing we relate to pleasure, and waning to pain. *Puruṣa* is thus analogous to the full moon.

S: Sukeśa admitting his ignorance appears noble.

G: It is a sign of learnedness, not seen much in the so-called learned of the present day. No one knows everything; admitting ignorance is not demeaning. The learned of the present day, especially academics, instead of admitting ignorance, mostly try to escape, evading problems. Real learnedness should not make one egotistic, must make one humble, as evident in Sukeśa. Pippalāda the Guru also is an exemplar of this humility; he asked the approaching seekers, "You live with me for an year, then ask me questions, if any; I shall answer if I happen to know." He, admitting his own limitations, did not assure them of answers to all their questions.

S: What is *anṛta*, translated as 'untruth'?

G: What is ultimately real is termed *satya* in Sanskrit; its oppsoite *asatya*. The real, as it unfolds itself as this world and its functional system, is called *ṛta*; its opposite *anṛta*. Those actions of ours in full harmony with *ṛta* are also termed *ṛta* and all else *anṛta*. To say something with something else in mind is *anṛta*; to tell lies is *anṛta*. No *anṛta* is more deceitful and despicable than pretending to know something and talking about it in a tone of authority. One who does it ruins himself as well as the hearer.

तस्मै स होवाच। इहैवान्तःशरीरे सोम्य स पुरुषो यस्मिन्नेताः षोडशकलाः प्रभवन्तीति ॥ २ ॥

tasmai sa hovāca । ihaivāntaḥ-śarīre somya sa puruṣo yasminn etāḥ ṣoḍaśa-kalāḥ prabhavanti iti ॥ 2 ॥

To him he (Pippalāda) said: Here indeed, within the body, O Dear, is that *puruṣa*. From Him arise these sixteen *kalā*s.

Seeker: Is this *puruṣa*, said to be 'within the body', what we call the soul?

Guru: The phrase 'within the body' is always construed by us by habit as meaning 'within one's own body', but prior to saying 'within the body' (*antaḥ śarīre*) it is also said 'here indeed' (*iha eva*); *iha* in Vedānta means 'in this whole world'. *Puruṣa* therefore is the live substance that underlies the body of the whole world, as gold underlies all ornaments.

S: What is meant by *śarīra*?

G: Used in the sense 'physical body', the word literally means 'that which perishes'. Everything in this world being perishable, their aggregate, this world, is the *śarīra*. *Puruṣa* is the live substance of this *śarīra*. The *Bhagavad Gītā*, defining *śarīra*, includes within it all that is conceivable in this world, from the grossest physical elements to the subtlest life principle (*cetanā*).

S: Why do the *kalās* have to arise from *puruṣa*?

G: This stanza suggestively summarises the first chapter wherein the theme discussed was the origin of beings, here replaced by *kalās*. Arising of *kalās* thus means the arising of beings. The origin of beings ultimately is *Brahman* itself, allegorically represented here as the *param puruṣa*. *Puruṣa* has to exist in some form or another, represented by *kalās*, just as gold has to exist in the form of ornaments.

स ईक्षांचक्रे। कस्मिन्नहमुत्क्रान्त उत्क्रान्तो भविष्यामि कस्मिन् वा प्रतिष्ठिते प्रतिष्ठास्यामीति ॥ ३ ॥

sa īkṣāṁcakre । kasminn aham utkrānta utkrānto bhaviṣyāmi kasmin vā pratiṣṭhite pratiṣṭhāsyāmi iti ॥ 3 ॥

He (the *puruṣa*) thought (of Himself): Whose departing makes me also depart? Whose settling down makes me also settle down?

Seeker: *Puruṣa* seems to ask himself a question.

Guru: It is simply a rhetorical question. Given that *Brahman* has necessarily to exist assuming the form of the world, the question arises, "Where does this form come from?" *Puruṣa* is, we know, the indweller of the *pura*, the city, the aggregate of the sixteen *kalās*. *Puruṣa* and *pura* cannot exist, one without the other. The origin of *pura* has not come to our attention yet. Where do the shapes of ornaments emerge from?

S: From gold.

G: That on the departing of all shapes, the gold also has to vanish, is an impossibility. So too, that on the departing of the body, the *pura*, the *puruṣa* also will have to vanish is an impossibility. *Puruṣa*, *ātmā* / *Brahman*, the one Reality, cannot exist other than in the form of the world. He therefore creates the sixteen *kalās*, his own body, the *pura*, from Himself, as stated in the next stanza.

S: How all the senses cease to function on the departing of the chief *prāṇa* was what was discussed in Chapter II. Can't we take this stanza as a restatement of it?

G: Yes. That way this stanza summarises in Chapter II. *Prāṇa*, the theme of Chapter III also is thus seen as not different from *puruṣa* or *Brahman* (*Ātman*).

स प्राणमसृजत। प्राणाच्छ्रद्धां खं वायुर्ज्योतिरापः पृथिवीन्द्रियं मनः।
अन्नमन्नाद्वीर्यं तपो मन्त्राः कर्मलोकाः लोकेषु च नाम च ॥ ४ ॥

sa prāṇaṁ asṛjata । *prāṇāc chraddhāṁ khaṁ vāyur*
jyotir āpaḥ pṛthivīndriyaṁ manaḥ । *annam annād vīryaṁ*
tapo mantrāḥ karma lokāḥ lokeṣu ca nāma ca ॥ 4 ॥

He created *prāṇa*; from *prāṇa* faith, space, air, fire, water, earth, sense-organs, mind and food; from food vitality, austerity, hymns, actions, worlds, and in the worlds, names too.

Seeker: No intention on the part of *puruṣa* to create all these was seen in the last stanza.

Guru: That intention was stated at the very beginning of the Upaniṣad where *puruṣa* assumed the form of Prajāpati. Pondering on his own being he discovered the impossibility of his existing without assuming the form of the world, the aggregate of the items enumerated in this stanza, not other than the sixteen *kalās*. No creation in fact takes place. The root *sṛj* from which is derived the word *asṛjata* (created) strictly means, to emanate, to well up, a process by which potential hidden in something becomes actualised. In philosophical terms this process is called 'becoming', and the substance that undergoes the process is 'being'. The emanation of the sixteen *kalās* — *prāṇa*, *śraddhā* (faith), space, air, fire, water, earth, sense-organs, mind, food, vitality, austerity, hymns, actions, world, names — is from Prajāpati himself and it ensures His own existence.

S: No particular order is seemingly followed in the enumeration of the *kalās*, the five gross elements apart. All the senses are telescoped into one, the four mental faculties into *manas*. Amd items such as austerity, hymns and actions do not fit in.

G: Bringing the entire range of worldly phenomena under sixteen categories being the intention, neither their contiguity no correlatedness is strictly cared for. Yet a contiguity is roughly followed: *prāṇa* was emanated from *puruṣa* first, items from *śraddhā* to food, from *prāṇa*, from food were originated vitality, austerity (*tapas*), hymns (*mantras*), actions (*karmas*), worlds and names.

S: Why was *prāṇa* originated first?

G: What the role of *prāṇa* is was seen in Chapter II and how *prāṇa* originated from *ātmā* in Chapter III. This stanza being a summarisation of Chapter III, and the *ātmā* of that chapter being identified with *param puruṣa* in this chapter, *prāṇa* first originating from *puruṣa* fits in with the scheme of the Upaniṣad as a whole.

S: How does *śraddhā*, one's faith in the word of one's Guru and of the scriptures, originate from *prāṇa*?

G: *Śraddhā* as one's faith in one's Guru and scriptures is not relevant in this context of emanation of the world from *puruṣa*, as there is no Guru-disciple relation involved. The faith relevant here therefore must be *puruṣa*'s faith in himself. *Puruṣa* must have the confidence of being able to emanate his own abode from himself in order to ensure his own existence; *prāṇa* must have the faith in himself of being able to keep up the coherence of the world. No confidence, no self-emanating and self-existence.

S: The five basic elements, sense-organs, mental faculties, are all familiar to us as constituents of living organisms, especially of human beings. Food is their sustaining factor.

G: Food is a principle more intimately related to *prāṇa* than other items. The *prāṇa* that works in nature causes the emanation of food from nature; the *prāṇa* that works in organisms causes the feeling of hunger. So intimately related are *prāṇa* and food that one would be meaningless and non-existent without the other. How vitality derives from food and how it is related to *prāṇa*, everyone knows.

S: How are *tapas* and vitality related?

G: You will get a direct answer if you try to practice *tapas* along with fasting.

S: How are *mantras*, emanations of food?

G: What underlies and controls the existence and function of the *kalās*, as pertaining to a whole, is knowledge; nay, knowledge is the underlying Reality in all of them. Knowledge finds expression through words; *mantras* are the expressions of the primordial knowledge — of the scriptures. They are neither expressible nor understandable while fasting, for want of vitality.

S: It should be in the same way that *karma* is related to food.

G: Yes. Words are verbal expressions of knowledge, *karmas* physical expression of knowledge. Pure Consciousness, being the essential content of the Self, the Reality underlying everything, *karma* is the creative urge in the Self for self-expression; it is not of individual beings or entities. The *Bhagavad Gītā* defines *karma* thus:

> That specific creative urge that causes the emanation of beings is named *karma*. — VIII. 3

The same *Gītā* verse says this *karma* is inherent in the one imperishable Reality, *Brahman*. *Brahman*, always having *karma* in it, is eternally active, and as active it is called *prakṛti*, loosely translated as 'nature'. Even the word *prakṛti* has involved in it *kṛti*, another word for *karma*. No *karma* finds expression in the absense of vitality derived from food.

S: Last of all come worlds and names. Could they be the fourteen worlds Hinduism believes in?

G: Such an interpretation need not be ruled out. Used also to mean 'people', the word *loka*, we know, literally means that which could be looked at. What can be looked at are forms; the aggregate of forms constitute the world (*loka*). Every form conceived by the human mind has been given a name; thus names stand for ideas as well. The world of names and ideas, and the world of forms are alike in magnitude, though unimaginably immense. One making the other comprehensible, the two are mutually dependent.

S: Food is given a central place among the *kalās*. Is it ordinary food alone that it signifies, or could we treat all sort of enjoyables as food?

G: The latter would be more appropriate.

S: The sixteen *kalās*, as poetical tradition has it, pertain to the moon. Is the moon relevant at all in this context?

G: Yes, it is. Desirous of creation, Prajāpati in the beginning brought out *prāṇa* and *rayī* from himself; *prāṇa* was then equated to the sun and *rayī*, later seen as consisting of everything phenomenal, was equated to the moon. The same phenomena are here reduced to sixteen *kalās*.

S: The *prāṇa* and *rayī* of the first chapter emerged from Prajāpati separate, whereas *prāṇa* forms part of the sixteen *kalās* representing *rayī* or the moon. Why this inconsistency?

G: This variance is owing to the difference between the two frames of reference.

S: What do you mean?

G: The theme of the first chapter was Prajāpati creating the world on his desiring progeny. The emanation of the world, *kalās*, from the *puruṣa* is not impelled by any such desire; his interest is only in self-existence. Prajāpati's desire was relative and conditioned, its actualisation depending on the mating of male and female, more earth-earthy in nature. The emanation of the *kalās* from *puruṣa*, wholly self-sustained, is unconditioned and non-relative in nature. Nothing that emerges from someone forms something else in essence; all continue to be his own *kalās*, integral part of him. The closed circle of the former context is contained within the ever open circle of the latter, the *prāṇa* of the former context is thus covered by the *rayī* of the latter.

It was with a creation-picture that the Upaniṣad began; its end also is with the same picture, but of a changed tone; the former more actual and the latter more virtual; the many pre-eminent in the former and the one pre-eminent in the latter. The problem with which the Upaniṣad began thus attains a new dimension and its answer a new finality, completing a full circle of thought. Unless this methodological peculiarity is noticed, the beauty of the Upaniṣad and the integrity of its vision remains a closed book to its students.

स यथेमा नद्यः स्यन्दमानाः समुद्रायणाः समुद्रं प्राप्यास्तं गच्छन्ति भिद्येते तासां नामरूपे समुद्र इत्येवं प्रोच्यते एवमेवास्य परिद्रष्टुरिमाः षोडशकलाः पुरुषायणाः पुरुषं प्राप्यास्तं गच्छन्ति; भिद्येते तासां नामरूपे पुरुष इत्येवं प्रोच्यते स एषोऽकलोऽमृतो भवति तदेष श्लोकः ।। ५ ।।

sa yathemā nadyaḥ syandamānāḥ samudrāyaṇāḥ

samudraṁ prāpyāstaṁ gacchanti bhidyete tāsāṁ nāma-rūpe samudra ity evaṁ procyate evam evāsya paridraṣṭur imāḥ ṣoḍaśa-kalāḥ puruṣāyaṇāḥ puruṣaṁ prāpyāstaṁ gacchanti; bhidyete tāsāṁ nāma-rūpe puruṣa ity evaṁ procyate sa eṣo'kalo'mr̥to bhavati tad eṣa ślokaḥ ॥ 5 ॥

Just as these flowing rivers heading for the ocean, on reaching it, disappear with their names and forms diffused, and are simply called ocean, even so, of this *puruṣa*, these sixteen *kalās*, heading for Him the perceiver, their names and forms diffused, are called simply the *puruṣa*, the *kalā*-less, the Immortal. As to it, there is this verse:

Seeker: That all rivers, on reaching the ocean, lose their identity and merge with the ocean, is an analogy easy to understand, but how the *kalās*, emanated from the *puruṣa*, go back and merge with Him is not clear.

Guru: The emergence of ornaments from gold does not imply the existence of ornaments apart from gold. So too is the world emanated from the *puruṣa*. The *puruṣa* and the *kalās* are inseparably one. The illusory impression that something new emerged might have been caused by the words, "From him arise these sixteen *kalās*". This shortcoming is immediately rectified by saying, the *kalās* go back to *puruṣa* and, merging with Him, lose their identity. What is real is the inseparability and non-duality of *puruṣa* and *kalās*.

S: Should we call this Reality, neither *puruṣa* nor *kalā*, *puruṣa* then?

G: Here we face the limitations of language, which are readily overcome by calling it *akalā*, the *kalā*-less. *Akalā* is also the opposite of *sakala*, one of the key concepts of Śaiva Siddhānta. Such an inseparable oneness of *puruṣa* and *kalās* alone is worth considering *amr̥ta*, the Immortal.

S: Could *kalās* merging back with *puruṣa* be treated as meaning that everything created, if created at all, returns to its source on dissolution.

G: Yes. Only then will the special methodological structure of this Upaniṣad, of ending where it began, become perfect. But such an interpretation can exist only where creation is taken for granted.

S: Could this stanza be considered as a condensation of Chapter IV?

G: Yes, of course, but in a rather indirect way. How the different states of consciousness merge with the one Substance-Consciousness was the theme of Chapter IV. Those states are replaced here with the *kalās*, their oneness with *puruṣa* comparable to the flowing of rivers into ocean.

अरा इव रथनाभौ कला यस्मिन् प्रतिष्ठिताः।
तं वेद्यं पुरुषं वेद यथा मा वो मृत्युः परिव्यथा इति ॥ ६ ॥

arā iva ratha-nābhau kalā yasmin pratiṣṭhitāḥ ।
taṁ vedyaṁ puruṣaṁ veda yathā mā vo mṛtyuḥ parivyathā iti ॥ 6 ॥

Wherein the *kalās* rest firm, like spokes on the hub of a wheel — know Him as the *puruṣa* to be known! Death thus disturbs you not!

Seeker: Is there any other intention than substantiating Pippalāda's own stand, in quoting this verse of a more ancient *ṛṣi*?

Guru: Yes, there is. What was taught so far in this Upaniṣad constitutes only the *śravaṇa* or hearing part. The seekers are expected to imbibe it and transform it into their own experience through *manana* (intense cogitation) and *nididhyāsana* (meditation). Pippalāda, instead of asking them directly to undergo these further steps, simply quotes the words of another authoritative *ṛṣi*; they say what is to be known is one *puruṣa* alone suggesting that the seekers are yet to know the real *puruṣa*. No Guru can go any further in teaching *Brahma-vidyā*; the experiential awareness is to be attained by the seekers on their own.

S: How do the river-ocean analogy and the hub-spoke analogy help the seeker to attain the Real?

G: Very dear to the Upaniṣadic *ṛṣis*, both the analogies show how the one and the many are really non-dual, the emphasis in the former on the meaninglessness of multiplicity of names and forms once the non-dual is attained, the latter stressing how the multiple entities that emanate from the One have their proper abode in the very same One. Such analogies could be added to any extent to give emphasis to one aspect or another of the mysterious non-duality. Still the seeker has to intensely cogitate and meditate on it before enlightenment is attained. The present two analogies help the seeker in his attainment, by being mutually complementary and mutually cancellable.

S: How?

G: *Amṛtatva* (immortality) was shown in the previous verse as the end-result of meditating with river-ocean analogy for an aid. 'Death thus disturbs you not' is the final result indicated here. Both the results really mean the same, but put, one as the positive attainment of a positive value — immortality — and the other as the negative process of avoiding death which is of negative value. The one meaning content of these two opposing statements, the real meaning intended to be conveyed, is neither of the two, but is ineffable.

S: Is this verse a summarisation of Chapter V?

G: Yes, of course. How the three limbs *A*, *U*, and *Ṁ* fit into the mono-syllable *AUṀ*, along with many other triple factors, was the theme of Chapter V. Such triple factors, in this verse, are replaced with the spokes of a wheel, and *AUṀ* with the hub of the wheel.

तान्‌ होवाचैतावदेवाहमेतत्‌ परं ब्रह्म वेद। नातः परमस्तीति ॥ ७ ॥

tān hovāca etāvad evāham etat paraṁ brahma veda ।
nātaḥ param asti iti ॥ 7 ॥

To them then Pippalāda said: This much only do I know of that Supreme *Brahman.* Nothing is there beyond this.

Seeker: Why did Pippalāda say, "This much only do I know?"

Guru: No *jñānin* claims to be a *jñānin*. No wise man claims to know everything. Wisdom makes them humble. Even from the very beginning Pippalàda's humility was evident.

S: He says, there is nothing beyond this. Did he mean that he did not know beyond this, or that there is nothing to be known beyond this?

G: From Pippalāda's point of view, he knew nothing beyond this; from the seeker's point of view, there is nothing beyond this to know.

ते तमर्चयन्तस्त्वं हि नः पिता योऽस्माकमविद्यायाः परं पारं तारयसीति। नमः परमऋषिभ्यो नमः परमऋषिभ्यः ॥ ८ ॥

te taṁ arcayantas tvaṁ hi naḥ pitā yo'smākam avidyāyāḥ paraṁ pāraṁ tārayasi iti। namaḥ parama ṛṣibhyo namaḥ parama ṛṣibhyaḥ ॥ 8 ॥

Praising him they said:
You are truly our father;
You are taking us across to the other shore of ignorance.
Adoration to the Supreme Seers!
Adoration to the Supreme Seers!

Seeker: Why are the *ṛṣis* in general adored instead of adoring Pippalāda?

Guru: The wisdom imparted so far by Pippalāda to the six seekers is not any theory or idea of his own; it is the eternal teaching handed down through a long line of *ṛṣis*. Pippalāda too received it by their grace, evident as it is from the oft repeated mention, "As to this there is this verse." It is therefore the long line of *ṛṣis* that deserves adoration, and not a particular *ṛṣi*. Such *ṛṣis* have always emerged at critical junctures of human history; we are hopeful that the same will happen in future too, to enlighten this wisdom, and to enlighten humanity.

शान्ति पाठः

ॐ भद्रं कर्णेभिः शृणुयाम देवाः भद्रं पश्येमाक्षभिर्यजत्राः।
स्थिरैरङ्गैस्तुष्टुवाꣳसस्तनूभिर् व्यशेम देवहितं यदायुः॥

स्वस्ति न इन्द्रो वृद्धश्रवाः स्वस्ति नः पूषा विश्ववेदाः।
स्वस्ति नस्तार्क्ष्यो अरिष्टनेमिः स्वस्ति नो बृहस्पतिर् दधातु॥

ॐ शान्तिः। शान्तिः। शान्तिः॥

oṁ bhadraṁ karṇebhiḥ śṛṇuyāma devāḥ
bhadraṁ paśyemākṣabhiryajatrāḥ ।
sthirair aṅgaistuṣṭuvām̐ sas tanūbhir
vyaśema devahitaṁ yadāyuḥ ॥

svasti na indro vṛddhaśravāḥ
svasti naḥ pūṣā viśvavedāḥ ।
svasti nas tārkṣyo ariṣṭanemiḥ
svasti no bṛhaspatir dadhātu ॥

oṁ śāntiḥ । *śāntiḥ* । *śāntiḥ* ॥

AUṀ May we, with our ears hear that which is auspicious, O gods.
And may we, habitually offering oblations, see with our eyes that which is auspicious.
With strong bodies, offering your praises, may we live our span of life destined to us by the gods.
May Indra of mature learning bestow well-being on us.
May Pūṣā (the sun), the knower of all, bestow well-being on us.
May Tārkṣya (Garuḍa), the annihilator of danger, bestow well-being on us.
May Bṛhaspati bestow well-being on us.

AUṀ Peace ! Peace ! Peace!

Glossary

Abhayam: Fearlessness. One of the aspects in which the knowledge of *Brahman* is experienced as a value.

Ādhibhautika-duḥkha: Sufferings caused by other beings.

Ādhidaivika-duḥkha: Sufferings caused by providence.

Adhyātma-sthūla-saṁkalpanā: A compound word coined by Narayana Guru to indicate how the one Reality, Consciousness in essence, by its own will, assumes the form of all concrete entities. Literally, 'the concretised will of the Self'.

Ādhyātmika duḥkha: Self-caused sufferings. See *ādhidaivika duḥkha*. and *ādhibhautika duḥkha*.

Advaita: Non-duality. The finally attained unitive vision, where vestiges of every shade of duality, such as one and the many, particular and universal, psychological and cosmological, have been transcended by one of philosophical vision.

Agni: Fire, a sacrificial fire.

Āhavanīyāgni: One of the three sacrificial fires. A consecrated fire taken from the householder's perpetual fire (see *gārhapatyāgni*).

Āhuti : Offering an oblation to a deity. Any solemn rite accompanied with oblations.

Ajāta-vāda : The theory that nothing new is born in this world. Only what already exists gets transformed.

Ākāśa : Space. That which gives room for everything to exist. Also called *vyoman*.

Akṣaram : The imperishable. Refers to the Ultimate Reality, *Brahman*.

Amṛta : Immortality or the Immortal Reality. Poetically imagined as the elixir in a golden pot that emerged from the Milk Ocean when the *deva*s and the *asura*s churned it together.

Amūrta: That which is abstract, like the beauty in a beautiful flower. Its opposite is *mūrta*, meaning the concrete.

Ānanda (*Ānandam*) : Bliss. To be understood in the context of the Good in Western philosophy as a supreme value. *Sat, cit* and *ānanda* are terms conjointly used to describe the Absolute (*Brahman*) in Vedānta. Concerning an individual being, it is to be understood as the value consciousness that enables one to evaluate his own experience either as pleasant or unpleasant.

Anna (*Annam*) : Food. That which could be enjoyed. Something is called *annam* because it is eaten and it eats beings. Even wisdom could be conceived as a sort of food.

Antarikṣa : Literally, that which is perceived in the middle. The middle world conceived in the Vedas as existing between the earth and heaven.

Antevāsin : One who dwells near. Term applied to a disciple who spends years in the household of the Guru, serving him and maintaining the sacrificial fires.

Apāna : One of the five vital functions, suggesting the downward movement of air in living bodies. The *Praśna Upaniṣad* conceives it as the vital function that effects excretion and emission.

Apara-Brahman: Lower *Brahman* as opposed to *para-Brahman*. The causal Reality conceived as appearing as all the effects.

Aparokṣa-anubhūti : Literally immediate experience. The intuitive experience of one's own identity with the Absolute or *Brahman*. The satisfaction of fulfilment of enquiry on one's finding the Reality searched for as oneself.

Asat : Non-existence, the non-existent, that which is morally void.

Āśrama : The four stages of human life, according to Indian tradition; namely, *brahmacarya* (studenthood), *gārhasthya* (householder's life), *vānaprastha* (a hermit's life), *saṁnyāsa* (a renunciate's life).

Ātmā (*Ātman*) : The self (from the root *āt*, to pervade). The invisible reality or substance that pervades any visible form. Often confused with *jīva*, the soul. Used in slightly altered senses according to the context. The simplest meaning of the word is 'I' or 'oneself'.

Ātmānanda: Self-happiness attained through knowing what really is one's own self-content.

Bhadram : The auspicious.

Bhāva : Becoming. Any manifest form of that which exists (*sat*). Derived from the root *bhū*, to become.

Brahmacarya : See *brahmacārin*.

Brahmacārī (*Brahmacārin*) : (from *Brahman*, the Absolute, and *cārin*, one who moves on). One who is moving on the path of *Brahman*. Name of one who is in the first stage of life as a student in a *gurukula*. Such a way of life is called *brahmacarya*. As a corollary, this kind of life would include such disciplines as continence as helpful to realisation. But sex is only one of the implied considerations in the discipline of a *brahmacārī*. As evidenced many times in the Upaniṣads, *ṛṣis* have been married and still able to walk the path of *Brahman*.

Brahma-jñānin : A knower of *Brahman*, the Absolute. The knower of *Brahman* becomes *Brahman* indeed.

Brahmaloka : The world of Brahmā, the Creator, or the world of *Brahman*, or the world conceived as *Brahman* become manifest.

Brahman : The Absolute. Literally, that which is always growing. Also the name of the chief priest in a fire-sacrifice.

Brahmānanda : Literally, the Bliss of *Brahman*. The ecstatic state in which one finds identity with *Brahman*.

Brahma-vidyā : The science of *Brahman* or the Absolute. Another name of Vedānta.

Bṛhaspati : The preceptor of gods.

Cakra : Wheel.

Camata : Firewood used for fire-sacrifices.

Caturvedī : One who admits all the four Vedas as authoritative scriptures. (See *trivedi*).

Cidākāśa : The consciousness-space.

Cid-ghana : That which is *cit*, Consciousness, in essence. That which is made up of *cit*.

Cit : Literally, consciousness. The essential content of the imperishable Reality pervading all the perishable and visible forms is pure Consciousness. Hence, *Brahman* is designated as *cit*. See *sat* and *ānanda* also.

Citta : The functional aspect of consciousness by which memories are stored up.

Devas : Vedic heavenly entities opposed to *asuras* (demons). Each of the *devas* (gods) represent the mysteriousness of a particular natural phenomenon.

Devatā : A deity. A god as understood in the context of adoration or worship. Every Vedic hymn has a deity who is praised, a *chanda* or a particular metre in which it is composed, and a *ṛṣi*, the seer who composed it.

Deva-yāna : The path of the gods. One of the two paths through which the departed souls supposedly go to the other world from where they will not return. Literally, the bright path. Also called *śukla-gati*, the white path. See *pitṛ-yāna*.

Dharma-śāstra : Scriptures of moral instruction.

Dhṛti : Firmness of mind.

Gārhapatyāgni : One of the three sacred fires perpetually maintained by a householder, which he receives from his father and transmits to his descendents and from which fires for sacrificial purposes are lighted.

Hṛt, hṛdaya : Heart.

Indra : The first of the gods of the Vedic heaven with Mitra, Varuṇa and other presiding deities of phenomenal aspects. Indra's heaven is where all desires are fulfilled, and where plenty pervails.

Iṣṭa-karma : Pious acts such as performing fire-sacrifices, worshipping deities and the like, contrasted with *pūrta karma* which are pious acts meant for public benefit, such as digging public wells, building camp sheds for travellers, planting shade trees and the like.

Īśvara : God; in the sense, the controller of everything.

Jagat : The world. Literally, that which is always on the move.

Jāgrat : Waking state.

Jātavedas : Fire. Literally, the knower of all that is born.

Jīva : The Sanskrit equivalent to soul. Often confused with *ātman*, the Self.

Jñānin : One who possesses *jñāna*. One who has attained enlightenment. *Jñāna* means Wisdom as contrasted with *karma* (works or rituals). *Jñāna-mārga* or the way of Wisdom gives primacy to reason and intuition.

Kalā : A minute part of anything. Also means, art.

Kāraṇa : Cause. Gold is cause and ornament is effect. What really exists is gold alone. Similarly, what really exists in the world is *Brahman* alone, which is its cause. This way of thinking is called *sat-kāraṇa- vāda* (theory giving primacy to cause). Indians distinguish two kinds of causes, viz., *upādāna-kāraṇa* (material cause) like clay for pots and *nimitta-kāraṇa* (incidental cause) like the potter and his tools.

Kāraṇa-bhāna : Specially used by Narayana Guru to denote that specific mode of consciousness at deep-sleep in which one is ignorant of everything.

Kāraṇa-śarīra : The body with the help of which consciousness remains fully ignorant in deep-sleep state.

Karma : All actions in general. Philosophically the creative urge inherent in the Imperishable Reality, causing the emergence of all manifest forms. In the Vedic context, the ritual of burnt sacrifice enjoined by the Vedas. As a religious belief of the Hindus, the incipient memory factors clinging to the souls as a result of their deeds in previous births. All are bound to enjoy or suffer the fruits of their deeds, and will have to reincarnate for this purpose. One might be accumulating more *karma*s in the new birth. This vicious chain of action goes on till one attains final release. Such *karma*s are divided into three categories — *sañcita-karma* (the actions accumulated in all the previous births), *āgāmī-karma* (fresh actions to be done in the present life-time) and *prārabdha-karma* (actions already initiated but the eating of their fruits is not finished with).

Kevala : Abstract Reality.

Mahimā : Greatness. Etymologically the quality of being worshippable.

Manana : Intense cogitation on what is heard from the Guru.

Manas : Mind. That which is constituted of *manas* is called *manomaya*. *Manas* consists of the questioning, doubting and imagining faculties of consciousness.

Manuṣya: Man; humankind. Literally, the descendents of Manu, the thinking being.

Māyā : Connotes a factor of epistemological and methodological importance in Śaṅkara's Vedānta especially, and in the Upaniṣadic lore generally. Whatever is postulated as the cause of the unreal, spoken of in the most generic of categorical terms in philosophy, as against theology, is to be laid at the door of *māyā*. It is the basis of duality or synergic antinomies. The nearset Western equivalent is the *Nagativitat* of Hegel's system.

Mukti (*Mokṣa*) : Final liberation. Literally, 'freedom'.

Mṛtyu : Death.

Mūrta : That which is concrete as against abstract. That which has distinct perceivable qualities.

Naraka : Hell.

Nididhyāsana : Meditation that results in the intuitive vision of non-duality.

Nirupādhika : The unconditioned as aganist *sopādhika*, the conditioned.

Nirviśeṣa : The attributeless.

Niṣkala : The partless.

Pañcīkaraṇa : The way the five basic elements supposedly are blended together so as to appear as actual physical elements.

Pāpa : Sin acquired through evil deeds.

Para-Brahman : The higher *Brahman*. Śaṅkara conceives of two aspects of *Brahman*. The lower *Brahman* (*Apara Brahman*) is the ultimate Reality having forms of the world for its attributes. The higher *Brahman* is attributeless, and hence is inconceivable.

Paramānanda: Supreme Happiness.

Parā-manas: The transcendental mind.

Phala-śruti: The envoy at the end of the text or of the chapters of scriptures, clarifying the benefit of acquiring the wisdom taught till then.

Piṇḍa: Literally, a lump or mass. The rice ball offered at the rituals to propitiate ancestors.

Pitṛ loka: The world of the departed souls (from *pitṛ*, manes or departed souls, and *loka*, the world).

Pitṛ-yāna: The path of the manes. One of the two paths through which the departed souls are supposed to travel to the other world from where they would have to return. Also called *kṛṣṇa-gati*, the black path. See *Deva-yāna*.

Prajā: That which is born. All living beings.

Prajāpati: The lord of *prajā*s, the Creator, another name of Brahmā.

Prajñāna-ghana: A synonymn for *cid-ghana*.

Prakaraṇa: A particular topic concentrated on in a particular part or section of a whole philosophical work.

Prakṛti: Nature. Literally, that which is active in the proper way.

Pralaya: The Deluge. Literally, proper dissolution.

Prāṇa: The vital breath. The functions of vital breath are identified as five, namely *prāṇa* (going upward), *apāna* (going downward), *vyāna* (that which takes vitality to every part of the body), *samāna* (that which keeps the balance of the body), and *udāna* (that which leaves the body at death).

Puṇya: Merit as against *pāpa* (sin).

Pūrta-karma: Any act of pious liberality, such as digging public wells, planting shade trees, building camp sheds for travellers. One of the two kinds of meritorious deeds.

Puruṣa: Literally, 'person'. The word is used both in the universal and particular senses. In the universal sense, He is the cosmic person who has the entire cosmos for his body. In this sense He is often called *virāṭ-puruṣa*.

Pūṣan: A synonym for the Sun. Literally, the nourisher.

Rājasa: Active.

Rayī: The bodily aspect of existence.

Retas: Semen.

Ṛṣi: A seer. A wise sage of ancient India, who lived generally in the seclusion of forests. They wrote all the hymns of the Vedas as well as the Upaniṣads. They were not necessarily monks and many of them had their wives living with them.

Śabda-prapañca: The world of words. Each entity in the physical world has a name in the world of words which is as extensive as the physical world.

Saccidānanda (*Sat* + *Cit* + *Ānanda*): Existence-Consciousness-Value experience, the only positive definition of *Brahman*. See *sat*, *cit* and *ānanda*.

Sādhaka: A spiritual seeker.

Sādhana: The spiritual discipline undergone for the attainment of a particular goal (*siddhi*).

Samāna: One of the five functional subdivisions of *prāṇa*. Its function is equalising the distribution of vitality and thus keeping up the balanced state of the organism.

Saṁskāra-vidhi: Any purificatory rite. Sixteen of them, including funeral rites, are to be gone through by a man in his life.

Śānti: Peacefulness. The one goal all aim at.

Śānti-pāṭha: Peace Invocation.

Śarīra: Literally that which perishes. The physical body or the visible form.

Sat: That which exists always. The subsisting reality in all the transient forms of the visible world, even as gold is the subsisting reality in all ornaments. *Brahman* as this subsisting Reality is designated as *sat*. See *ānanda* and *cit* also.

Sat-kāraṇa-vāda: The theory that cause alone is Real and all effects are mere superimpositions on *sat*, and therefore all appearances are unreal. This is the theory of Śaṅkara.

Saṭ-kārya-vāda: The theory that effect is as real as cause—Rāmanuja's theory.

Siddhi: Attainment. Supra-mundane attainments gained through certain yogic practices. Eight such attainments are referred to by Patañjali in his *Yoga-Sūtras*.

Śiva: Literally, the auspicious. The ancient hero-god, of prehistorical times, associated with radical virility and renunciation. He is an unconventional god like Dionysius, wearing skins and dancing in ecstasy, drunk with cosmic consciousness. He is the most ancient and the most important figure of the Indian pantheon, and occupies his seat in Banaras in the plains, and Kailāsa in the Himalayas.

Śivam: The auspicious.

Sphoṭa: The name of the Indian theory of semantics. Literally, bursting out. Meaning bursts out in mind just on hearing the utterance of a word.

Śraddhā: One of the prerequisites on the part of a seeker. Willingness to have full faith in the truthfulness of the word of the Guru and of the scriptures. A necessary stepping stone for *manana*.

Śravaṇa: Hearing attentively the words of instruction directly from a Guru.

Śrī: The prosperous. Another name of Lakṣmī, the goddess of prosperity.

Sthūla-bhāna: The concretised manifestation of Consciousness, the Reality, resulting in the experience of the gross (*sthūla*) world.

Sthūla-bhūta: Gross physical elements. It emerges as a result of the *pañcīkaraṇa* (see) of the subtle elements.

Sthūla-śarīra: The gross body with the help of which consciousness in its waking state becomes aware of the gross world.

Sukha: Another word for *ānanda*.

Sūkṣma-bhāna: That functional mode of consciousness because of which the subtle factors such as mind and sense-organs, their objects and vital functions emerge.

Sūkṣma-śarīra: The subtle body with the help of which consciousness creates and enjoys dreams.

Suṣupti: Deep-sleep.

Svāhā: The last word with which all *mantras* recited while performing fire-sacrifices end. According to belief, the first word uttered by the Creator while making an oblation (*sva + aha*). Svāhā is also considered the name of the wife of the Fire-God, Agni. If grammatical rules are not strictly followed, it could also be taken to mean, 'thus it has been said correctly' (from *su*, well, and *āha*, has been said).

Svarga: The Vedic heaven or Paradise, inhabited by *devas* (gods) whose chief is Indra.

Taijasa: Name of the state of consciousness in which one dreams. Literally, the bright one.

Tamas: Dark-inert.

Tapas: Austere self-discipline. Literally, 'heating up'.

Tejas: Brightness, fire.

Trivedī: One who considers the three Vedas (*Ṛgveda, Yajus, Sāma*) alone as authoritative. (See *cadurvedi*).

Turīya: Literally, the fourth. The transcendental state of Consciousness in which the *triputi* merges in the all engulfing Self-radiance. Narayana Guru defines it as, 'to know that which is bottomless and topless, from top to bottom'.

Udāna: One of the functional aspects of *prāṇa*. Its function is making one think of higher values.

Upaniṣad: Wisdom texts appended to the Vedas. Also called Vedānta as it appears at the end of the Vedas, and *jñāna-kāṇḍa* as it deals with wisdom. The word literally means 'to sit nearby and below' (*upa*=just below, *ni* = nearby, *ṣat* = to sit down). The name indicates a disciple sitting beside a *guru*. The word also means, 'the secret teaching'. The Upaniṣads teach the philosophy of *Brahman*, the Absolute. The ten major Upaniṣads are *Īśa, Kena, Kaṭha, Praśna, Muṇḍaka, Māṇḍūkya, Taittirīya, Aitareya, Chāndogya* and *Bṛhadāraṇyaka*.

Vaiśvānara: Name of consciousness in the waking state. Literally the universal man, or man's state in which he relates himself with the universe.

Vāsanā: Incipient memory factors that are inborn in individuals. Such unconscious factors decide to a great extent how one behaves in life.

Veda (Vedas): The earliest of the Indian scriptures, collected into four volumes, named the *Ṛgveda, Yajurveda, Sāmaveda,* and *Adharvaveda*. They praise gods like Indra, Varuṇa, Mitra and other phenomenal gods of nature. They were later overcome by the Upaniṣads. The word *veda* means knowledge. The Vedas generally stand for rituals (*karma*).

Vedānta: When the Vedic teachings had been revalued in philosophical terms by later *ṛṣis* (sages), a body of literature called Vedānta arose in the history of Indian thought. These often go contrary to the Vedic tendencies of rituals and obligations, announcing freedom and stressing Self-reaslisation. Later we find Śaṅkara, Rāmānuja and Madhva, referred to as three typical Vedāntic philosophers, although the Gurus of the Vedāntic line (*paramparā*) are many. (See also Upaniṣad).

Vidyā: Knowledge. That by which one understands the Real as the Real and the unreal as the unreal.

Vijñāna: Any specific or applied form of knowledge or wisdom.

Viraja: The passionless; the state in which *rajo-guṇa* is as if absent.

Virāṭ-puruṣa: See *puruṣa*.

Viṣṇu: The second of the trinity of the Hindu Pantheon of which Brahmā, the Creator is the first and Maheśvara or Śiva the last. Śiva is also the Destroyer. Viṣṇu is considered the preserver, although each of the three is preserver and destroyer as well. This shows the fusing together of the cosmological and psychological currents of religious thought in India.

Viśva: The cosmos. Literally, 'the all'.

Viśva-rūpa: The cosmic figure or form.

Viśva-vīrya: Cosmic creative urge. Equivalent to the *élan vital*.

Vrata: Any religious vow.

Vrātya: One who ignores purificatory rites.

Vṛddha-śravaḥ: One of matured understanding.

Vyāna: One of the functional aspects of *prāṇa*. Its function according to the *Praśna Upaniṣad* is distributing vitality to every part of the body through its countlessly branching nervous and circulatory system.

Yajamāna: A person who employs priests to perform fire-sacrifice for his sake. A person who performs a regular sacrifice and pays its expenses.

Yajatra: One who constantly maintains the sacrificial fire.

Yajña: Any sacrificial offering.

Yoga: (from the root *yuj*, to join). Psychic union of oneself with the Self, just as an ornament finds its oneness with gold. As a contemplative method of self-enquiry, the way of expressing an inexpressible reality by allowing it to be viewed from two opposite sides and leaving the unitive meaning to be understood by the reader or seeker. For example, 'attaining immortality' and 'crossing over death' are two expressions meaning the same. But these two expressions are opposite in nature. They have in between them a meaning that cannot be expressed as it is.

Different systems of *yoga* have been developed in India, each giving emphasis to a particular pair to be joined together. Patañjali's *Yoga-Sūtras* is the basic source book on *Yoga*. Patañjali's system is also known as *Rāja Yoga*. The names *Haṭha Yoga*, *Karma Yoga*, *Jñāna Yoga*, *Bhakti Yoga* are popular. Each of the eighteen chapters of the *Bhagavad-Gītā* is also named a *Yoga*. The *Bhagavad-Gītā* itself claims to be a *Yoga-Śāstra* (textbook on the science of *Yoga*).

Yoga-buddhi: The awareness attained by the method of *Yoga* (See *Yoga*).

Index